The Billionaire's Blueprint

The Billionaire's Blueprint

Matthew Petchinsky

1

The Billionaire's Blueprint: Unlocking Wealth Through Action

By: Matthew Petchinsky

Disclaimer

The information provided in *The Billionaire's Blueprint: Unlocking Wealth Through Action* is for educational and informational purposes only. This book is not intended to serve as financial, legal, tax, investment, accounting, medical, or professional advice of any kind. The author and publisher are not licensed financial advisors, certified public accountants, attorneys, brokers, or fiduciaries, and no portion of this book should be interpreted as personalized guidance tailored to your individual circumstances.

All strategies, concepts, examples, case studies, action plans, income models, and wealth-building frameworks discussed in this book are presented as general educational principles. Financial outcomes depend on numerous variables including, but not limited to, market conditions, geographic location, economic climate, access to capital, timing, risk tolerance, personal skill level, discipline, execution quality, regulatory compliance, and unforeseen external factors. Because these factors vary significantly between individuals, no guarantee is made that you will achieve similar results, specific income levels, business growth, investment returns, or wealth milestones by applying the methods described.

Any references to income figures, revenue targets, net worth levels, business valuations, or examples of financial success are illustrative only. They are not promises or representations of typical earnings. Wealth accumulation involves risk, including the potential loss of capital. Business ventures may fail. Investments may decrease in value. Markets may fluctuate. Regulatory environments may change. You accept full responsibility for any decisions you make based on the information presented in this book.

Before making financial, investment, tax, business formation, debt restructuring, real estate, securities, cryptocurrency, lending, partnership, or capital allocation decisions, you are strongly encouraged to consult with licensed professionals who can evaluate your specific situation. Acting without proper professional counsel may expose you to financial, legal, or regulatory risk.

Nothing in this book constitutes an offer to sell, a solicitation to buy, or a recommendation regarding any specific security, investment vehicle, financial instrument, business entity, partnership structure, or income-generating opportunity. The author does not provide investment advisory services and does not assume any fiduciary responsibility to the reader.

The discussions related to entrepreneurship, risk-taking, leverage, scaling, asset acquisition, debt management, taxation strategy, and wealth psychology are presented as conceptual frameworks for educational purposes. Implementation of these ideas may involve substantial risk. You are solely responsible for performing due diligence, verifying legal compliance, understanding regulatory obligations, and assessing personal risk exposure before taking action.

The author and publisher disclaim any liability for losses, damages, business interruptions, missed opportunities, lost profits, legal penalties, or other consequences resulting directly or indirectly from the use or misuse of the material contained in this book. By reading this book, you acknowledge that you are responsible for your own financial decisions and outcomes.

This book may reference third-party tools, services, technologies, business models, or financial structures. Such references are for informational context only and do not constitute endorsement, sponsorship, or affiliation unless explicitly stated. The author is not responsible for the performance, legality, or outcomes associated with third-party entities.

Past performance, whether discussed directly or indirectly, is not indicative of future results. Economic environments change. Market cycles shift. Opportunities evolve. What works in one season of the economy may not work in another. Strategic adaptation and informed decision-making are essential.

By continuing to read this book, you agree that you understand these terms and accept full responsibility for your actions, choices, financial risks, and results. The purpose of this work is to provide educational insight into wealth-building philosophy and disciplined execution—not to replace professional counsel or to guarantee financial success.

Introduction: The Psychology of Wealth, Conquering Fear, and the First Steps Toward Financial Independence

Wealth is not an accident. It is not luck. It is not reserved for a chosen few who were born into privilege or stumbled into the right opportunity at the perfect time. Wealth begins as a psychological shift long before it ever becomes a financial reality. It begins in the mind—long before it appears in a bank account.

Most people are not financially limited by opportunity. They are limited by conditioning.

From childhood, many are taught to seek security over growth. To avoid risk instead of mastering it. To pursue comfort rather than calculated expansion. We are trained to earn income, not to build assets. To work harder, not necessarily smarter. To save cautiously, but rarely to multiply boldly. The psychology of wealth challenges this conditioning at its core.

Before you can earn differently, you must think differently.

Before you can build differently, you must see differently.

Before you can act boldly, you must understand why you hesitate.

The Internal Battle: Fear vs. Expansion

The greatest obstacle between you and financial independence is not the market. It is not inflation. It is not competition. It is fear.

Fear of failure.
Fear of losing money.
Fear of judgment.
Fear of looking foolish.
Fear of success.
Fear of outgrowing your current environment.

Failure, in particular, holds immense psychological power. Many people would rather stay financially stagnant than risk visible defeat. Yet every billionaire, every entrepreneur, every investor who built significant wealth has a history of missteps, recalculations, and reinvention. Failure is not the opposite of wealth—it is often the tuition paid for it.

The difference between those who remain stuck and those who rise is not perfection. It is tolerance for discomfort.

Wealth builders develop emotional resilience before they develop financial leverage. They understand that losses are data. Mistakes are feedback. Delays are redirection. Rejection is filtration. Instead of asking, "What if I fail?" they ask, "What will I learn if I do?"

Fear shrinks when action begins.

The Wealth Identity Shift

Financial independence does not begin with income—it begins with identity.

If you internally identify as someone who "struggles with money," "is bad at business," or "never seems to get ahead," your actions will subconsciously reinforce that narrative. Identity drives behavior. Behavior produces outcomes. Outcomes reinforce identity.

To break the cycle, the identity must shift first.

A wealth-oriented identity does not mean pretending to be rich. It means thinking like an asset builder rather than a paycheck earner. It means:

- Seeing opportunities instead of obstacles
- Thinking in decades, not days
- Valuing ownership over consumption
- Prioritizing skill acquisition over entertainment
- Understanding leverage instead of trading time for money indefinitely

This shift is subtle but profound. When your identity changes, your standards change. When your standards change, your decisions change. When your decisions change consistently, your financial trajectory changes.

Action Over Information

We live in an era of infinite information and minimal execution.

Podcasts. Courses. Videos. Threads. Strategies. Blueprints. Systems.

Yet information alone does not create wealth. Applied action does.

Many individuals consume wealth content daily but hesitate to make their first move. They wait for perfect timing. They wait for more savings. They wait for more confidence. They wait for certainty.

But certainty is rarely available before action.

Financial independence begins with imperfect movement. The first business idea may not scale. The first investment may not perform optimally. The first attempt at negotiating income may feel uncomfortable. But forward motion compounds faster than hesitation.

You do not need a billion-dollar idea to begin.

You need a first step.

The Practical First Moves

Psychology fuels momentum—but action builds structure. This book is designed to merge both.

The first practical steps toward financial independence are rarely glamorous. They are foundational:

1. **Financial Awareness** – Understanding where your money flows, what drains it, and what builds it.
2. **Skill Expansion** – Identifying marketable skills that increase earning power.
3. **Income Leverage** – Moving from single-source dependency toward diversified streams.
4. **Asset Thinking** – Shifting focus from consumption to acquisition.
5. **Risk Calibration** – Learning to measure risk intelligently instead of avoiding it entirely.

Financial independence is not a single breakthrough moment. It is a series of disciplined, consistent actions that compound over time.

Compounding works in money.

It also works in habits.

It works in courage.

It works in reputation.

It works in momentum.

Redefining Wealth

Wealth is often misunderstood as luxury alone. But true financial independence is autonomy.

The ability to control your time.
The ability to choose your work.
The ability to weather economic downturns without panic.
The ability to create opportunities instead of waiting for them.

Money, in this sense, becomes a tool—not a trophy.

This blueprint is not about fantasy. It is about structure. It is about psychological alignment with disciplined execution. It is about recognizing that wealth is built intentionally, strategically, and persistently.

The Decision Point

Every financial journey begins with a decision.

Not a dramatic announcement.
Not a sudden windfall.
Not a viral breakthrough.

A decision.

A decision to stop operating from fear.
A decision to accept responsibility for financial growth.
A decision to act before you feel fully ready.
A decision to build, not just earn.

The psychology of wealth is not mystical. It is practical. It is trainable. It is built through repetition of aligned actions.

You do not need permission to begin.
You do not need perfect conditions.
You do not need a billionaire background.

You need clarity.
You need courage.
You need movement.

This book will guide you through the mindset, structure, and execution principles required to unlock wealth through action. The blueprint is not theoretical—it is operational.

The question is not whether wealth is possible.

The question is whether you are ready to think, decide, and act differently than before.

Your first step begins now.

Chapter 1: The Wealth Mindset

Beliefs Are Financial Blueprints

Every financial result you experience today is connected to a belief you accepted yesterday. Beliefs act as invisible architecture. They shape what you attempt, what you tolerate, what you avoid, and what you believe is possible. If you believe money is scarce, your decisions will be defensive. If you believe opportunity is abundant, your decisions will be expansive.

Most people never consciously choose their financial beliefs. They inherit them. Family conversations, childhood stress about bills, cultural narratives about "rich people," and past personal failures all contribute to subconscious programming. Over time, these ideas solidify into unquestioned truths. You may think you are making rational financial decisions, but in reality, you are reinforcing deeply embedded narratives.

A person who believes "money is hard to make" will unconsciously overlook simple opportunities. A person who believes "wealth requires unethical behavior" may sabotage growth when success begins to appear. A person who believes "I am not good with money" will avoid financial education entirely. These beliefs are not facts—they are stories repeated long enough to feel true.

The wealth mindset begins with awareness. Before you can change outcomes, you must examine assumptions. You must identify which beliefs serve you and which restrict you. The moment you question a limiting belief, you loosen its grip.

Financial abundance is not just about strategy. It is about internal alignment. When beliefs support growth, actions become more decisive. When actions become decisive, results begin to shift.

Scarcity vs. Abundance Thinking

Scarcity thinking focuses on limitation. It assumes there is not enough—money, opportunity, clients, jobs, resources, or luck. It creates competition rooted in fear rather than innovation rooted in value. Scarcity narrows vision and shortens time horizons.

Abundance thinking does not deny challenges. It reframes them. It recognizes that wealth can be created, expanded, and multiplied. Abundance sees collaboration where scarcity sees rivalry. It sees possibility where scarcity sees threat.

Scarcity often stems from survival conditioning. If you grew up witnessing financial instability, your nervous system may equate risk with danger. Even when circumstances improve, the emotional memory remains. This is why some individuals self-sabotage when income increases—they subconsciously return to what feels familiar.

Abundance thinking is built intentionally. It is not naive optimism. It is strategic confidence. It acknowledges risk but focuses on value creation. Instead of asking, "What if there isn't enough?" it asks, "How can I create more?"

When you operate from abundance, you invest in skill development. You pursue long-term assets. You build networks. You look for scalable systems instead of one-time wins. Your energy shifts from protection to expansion.

Identity and Financial Self-Concept

Your financial self-concept determines your income ceiling. If you see yourself as "middle class," "struggling," or "bad with numbers," you unconsciously maintain behaviors that reinforce that identity. Identity drives standards, and standards drive results.

A wealth mindset requires identity evolution. This does not mean pretending to have money you do not possess. It means adopting the habits, language, and decision-making patterns of someone who builds wealth. Identity change precedes income change.

If you identify as an investor, you begin to analyze assets differently. If you identify as an entrepreneur, you notice inefficiencies in markets. If you identify as a value creator, you focus on solutions rather than complaints. Identity directs attention, and attention shapes opportunity.

This shift is uncomfortable at first. Growth disrupts familiarity. You may feel imposter syndrome. You may question your worthiness. But identity is not static. It evolves through consistent behavior aligned with a new standard.

The more you act like someone building wealth, the more natural it becomes. Eventually, your identity and your financial trajectory align.

Emotional Mastery and Money Decisions

Money is emotional. Markets are emotional. Spending is emotional. Investing is emotional. Fear and greed drive entire economies. If you cannot regulate emotion, you cannot manage wealth effectively.

Fear leads to inaction. Panic leads to poor decisions. Overconfidence leads to reckless risk. Emotional mastery does not mean suppressing feelings. It means recognizing them without letting them dictate behavior.

When investments fluctuate, disciplined individuals evaluate data. Reactive individuals sell from panic. When opportunities arise, confident individuals calculate risk. Fearful individuals hesitate until the window closes. Emotional control creates strategic advantage.

Wealth builders cultivate delayed gratification. They understand that short-term discomfort often produces long-term stability. They choose investments over impulse purchases. They choose education over entertainment. They choose growth over comfort.

Emotional resilience strengthens financial resilience. The stronger your internal stability, the more consistent your external results.

The Power of Repetition and Mental Conditioning

The mind responds to repetition. Thoughts repeated frequently become beliefs. Beliefs reinforced consistently become identity. Identity shapes destiny.

If you repeatedly say, "I can't afford it," your brain searches for limitation. If you ask, "How can I afford it?" your brain searches for solutions. Language influences cognition. Cognition influences behavior.

Mental conditioning involves conscious repetition of empowering beliefs. Affirmations alone are insufficient without action, but they direct focus. Visualization prepares the brain for opportunity. Consistent exposure to wealth-building environments normalizes success.

Surroundings matter. Conversations matter. Content consumption matters. If you constantly absorb negativity about markets, your outlook narrows. If you engage with growth-oriented thinkers, your thinking expands.

Rewiring your wealth mindset requires daily reinforcement. Small adjustments compound. Just as investments grow over time, so do mental patterns.

From Thought to Action

A wealth mindset is incomplete without execution. Positive thinking without movement produces frustration. The purpose of mental rewiring is to fuel strategic action.

Once beliefs align with growth, you begin making bolder decisions. You seek skill acquisition. You explore scalable opportunities. You negotiate confidently. You allocate resources intentionally.

Action builds evidence. Evidence strengthens belief. The cycle reinforces itself. Each small financial win—saving consistently, increasing income, making a smart investment—confirms your new identity.

Momentum transforms mindset from theory into reality. With each disciplined action, fear decreases and confidence expands.

The wealth mindset is not a single breakthrough moment. It is a daily practice. It is choosing growth repeatedly until it becomes natural.

Exercises to Rewire Your Wealth Mindset

Exercise 1: Limiting Belief Audit

Step 1: Write down every negative belief you hold about money. Do not filter. Include phrases you heard growing up.

Step 2: Identify the origin of each belief (family, culture, personal failure, media).

Step 3: Challenge each belief with objective evidence. Ask: Is this universally true?

Step 4: Rewrite each limiting belief into an empowering alternative.

Step 5: Read the empowering statements aloud daily for 30 days while taking one small financial action aligned with them.

Exercise 2: Abundance Exposure Protocol

Step 1: Replace 30 minutes of daily passive consumption with financial education or wealth-building content.

Step 2: Identify one individual who embodies financial discipline and study their habits.

Step 3: Track daily examples of value creation you observe in markets.

Step 4: Practice asking solution-focused questions when financial challenges arise.

Step 5: Reflect weekly on changes in your perception of opportunity.

Exercise 3: Identity Alignment Drill

Step 1: Define the financial identity you are building (Investor, Entrepreneur, Asset Builder).

Step 2: List five habits this identity practices consistently.

Step 3: Implement one habit immediately and schedule the others.

Step 4: Remove one behavior that contradicts your desired identity.

Step 5: Track progress for 60 days and evaluate behavioral shifts.

Journal Prompts

1. What money beliefs did I inherit that may no longer serve me?
2. When did I first associate money with fear or stress?
3. What would my financial life look like if scarcity were no longer my default mindset?
4. How do I react emotionally when facing financial risk?
5. What identity shift would most dramatically increase my earning capacity?
6. Where have I sabotaged financial growth in the past?
7. What habits reinforce abundance in my daily routine?
8. What environments elevate my financial thinking?
9. How can I practice delayed gratification more consistently?
10. What small action can I take this week to reinforce my new wealth mindset?

Closing Reflection

Your financial life mirrors your internal narrative. Change the narrative, and the trajectory shifts. Wealth is not reserved for the fearless—it is built by those willing to examine fear, challenge belief, and act anyway.

The wealth mindset is not about fantasy. It is about disciplined thinking aligned with consistent execution. Each belief you reshape becomes a structural beam in your financial foundation.

The journey toward financial independence begins within. When your thoughts align with growth, your actions follow. When your actions align with discipline, results compound.

This is the first step in building wealth through action.

Chapter 2: Building the Millionaire Foundation

Financial Clarity: Knowing Your Numbers

A strong financial foundation begins with clarity. You cannot build wealth on confusion. Many people avoid looking closely at their numbers because it triggers discomfort, but avoidance creates fragility. Wealth builders confront reality directly. They know exactly what comes in, what goes out, what they owe, and what they own.

Financial clarity starts with a complete income and expense inventory. This includes fixed costs, variable spending, subscriptions, debt payments, and irregular expenses. When you document everything, patterns emerge. You begin to see leaks in your financial structure—small, repetitive costs that erode long-term wealth potential.

Clarity also includes understanding your net worth. List all assets—cash, investments, business equity, property—and subtract liabilities such as loans and credit balances. This single number becomes your baseline. It is not a judgment. It is a starting point.

Without clarity, budgeting becomes guesswork. Investing becomes risky. Skill development becomes disconnected from financial goals. Clarity aligns strategy with reality.

When you know your numbers, you regain control. Financial awareness shifts money from a source of anxiety into a measurable system you can improve.

Strategic Budgeting for Growth

Budgeting is often misunderstood as restriction. In truth, it is allocation. A millionaire foundation requires intentional distribution of resources. Every dollar must have a purpose—whether it is stability, growth, protection, or opportunity.

Start with essentials: housing, utilities, food, insurance, transportation. These form your stability layer. Stability ensures that your foundation is not constantly threatened by minor disruptions.

Next comes growth allocation. This includes savings, investments, business reinvestment, and skill acquisition. Growth spending is not optional; it is required. Without consistent allocation toward assets, financial independence remains theoretical.

A disciplined budget also creates an emergency reserve. Three to six months of essential expenses protects against sudden disruptions. This buffer reduces fear-based decision-making and increases strategic flexibility.

When budgeting becomes proactive instead of reactive, money flows with intention. You are no longer wondering where it went—you are directing where it goes.

Investment Literacy and Asset Accumulation

A millionaire foundation is built on assets, not income alone. Income pays bills. Assets generate freedom. The transition from earner to owner is critical.

Investment literacy begins with understanding risk tolerance, time horizon, and diversification. Different asset classes behave differently—equities, real estate, businesses, intellectual property, and cash reserves each serve distinct roles.

Compounding is the most powerful force in wealth building. When returns are reinvested, growth accelerates. Time amplifies consistency. The earlier and more consistently you invest, the greater the multiplier effect.

Diversification reduces volatility. It spreads exposure across multiple vehicles, minimizing the impact of any single downturn. Millionaire foundations are resilient because they are structured across multiple streams.

Investment literacy is not about chasing trends. It is about disciplined allocation, patience, and data-driven decision-making.

Skill Development as Capital

Skills are assets. They increase earning capacity and create leverage. In the early stages of wealth building, skill development often produces the highest return on investment.

Identify high-demand skills within markets—communication, negotiation, digital literacy, management, sales, coding, financial analysis. Skills that solve problems create income expansion.

Skill stacking multiplies opportunity. When complementary skills intersect, they create unique value. For example, combining technical knowledge with communication expertise enhances leadership potential.

Continuous education sustains relevance. Markets evolve. Industries shift. The foundation must adapt. Skill development is ongoing, not a one-time event.

When you treat skills as capital, you prioritize growth. Each new competency strengthens your financial architecture.

Income Expansion and Diversification

Relying on a single income source creates vulnerability. A millionaire foundation integrates diversification early. This does not require immediate complexity—it begins with incremental expansion.

Primary income should be optimized first. Negotiate raises. Improve performance. Increase productivity. Strong primary income accelerates investment capacity.

Secondary streams may include freelance work, digital products, consulting, dividends, rental income, or small business ventures. Each additional stream reduces dependency.

Diversification is strategic, not scattered. Each new stream should align with skill sets and long-term goals. Expansion without focus leads to burnout.

As streams stabilize, reinvest profits into assets. This converts active effort into passive growth over time.

Risk Management and Protection

A foundation must be protected. Wealth accumulation without protection exposes you to unnecessary setbacks.

Insurance—health, property, liability—forms a defensive layer. Estate planning and basic legal structures reduce long-term vulnerability. Protection ensures that growth is not undone by preventable risks.

Risk management also includes disciplined decision-making. Avoid high-leverage speculation without education. Avoid overexposure to volatile investments.

Maintain liquidity. Cash reserves provide opportunity and security. They allow you to act when markets shift.

A millionaire foundation balances offense and defense. Growth and protection work together to sustain momentum.

Exercises for Building Your Foundation

Exercise 1: Financial Blueprint Mapping

Step 1: Document all income sources and categorize expenses.

Step 2: Calculate net worth by subtracting liabilities from assets.

Step 3: Identify three unnecessary expenses and reallocate funds toward growth.

Step 4: Set a monthly savings percentage goal.

Step 5: Review progress at the end of each month.

Exercise 2: Skill Capital Assessment

Step 1: List current skills that generate income.

Step 2: Identify three high-demand skills aligned with your goals.

Step 3: Choose one skill to develop over the next 90 days.

Step 4: Allocate weekly learning hours.

Step 5: Apply the skill in a real-world context before the 90-day period ends.

Exercise 3: Investment Strategy Draft

Step 1: Define your financial goals and time horizon.

Step 2: Assess risk tolerance honestly.

Step 3: Research three asset classes suitable for your goals.

Step 4: Open or optimize an investment account aligned with your strategy.

Step 5: Commit to consistent contributions, regardless of short-term market fluctuations.

Journal Prompts

1. What does financial stability mean to me personally?
2. Where is my money currently leaking without purpose?
3. What asset class aligns most closely with my long-term vision?
4. Which skill could dramatically increase my earning power?
5. How comfortable am I with calculated risk?
6. What habits weaken my financial foundation?
7. What habits strengthen it consistently?
8. How diversified is my income today?
9. What protective measures do I need to implement immediately?
10. What would my financial life look like in five years if I executed consistently?

Closing Reflection

A millionaire foundation is not built overnight. It is constructed deliberately, layer by layer. Clarity creates structure. Budgeting directs flow. Investments multiply effort. Skills expand capacity. Diversification strengthens resilience. Protection sustains progress.

The foundation determines the ceiling. Strengthen it, and growth becomes sustainable. Neglect it, and expansion collapses under pressure.

This chapter is about structure, discipline, and preparation. With a solid base in place, wealth is no longer a distant aspiration—it becomes an engineered outcome.

The foundation is set. Now momentum can begin.

Chapter 3: Crafting Passive Income Streams

Understanding the Passive Income Philosophy

Passive income is often misunderstood as effortless money. In reality, it is front-loaded effort that produces recurring rewards. The goal is not to avoid work entirely but to decouple income from constant active labor. Instead of trading hours for dollars indefinitely, you build systems that continue producing value long after the initial work is complete.

The passive income philosophy begins with leverage. Leverage can come from capital, technology, intellectual property, or systems. When leveraged correctly, a single effort can generate income repeatedly. Writing a book once and earning royalties for years is leverage. Investing capital and receiving dividends is leverage. Building software that serves thousands without additional manual labor is leverage.

Time is the most valuable asset you possess. Passive income allows you to reclaim it. When income streams operate independently of your daily presence, you gain flexibility. You can reinvest time into skill development, new ventures, family, health, or strategic thinking.

True passive income still requires management. Monitoring performance, updating systems, and optimizing returns are part of the process. However, these efforts are periodic rather than constant. That difference is transformative.

The ultimate objective is financial autonomy. Passive income creates stability and scalability. It turns wealth building from survival into strategy.

The Foundation Before Automation

Before pursuing passive streams, ensure your financial foundation is stable. Emergency reserves, disciplined budgeting, and basic investment literacy reduce pressure. When survival stress is high, decision-making deteriorates. Stability provides clarity.

Passive income requires patience. It often takes months or years before streams reach meaningful scale. Without a financial cushion, many abandon promising systems prematurely. The foundation supports long-term thinking.

Debt management is also critical. High-interest debt erodes returns. Prioritize eliminating liabilities that outweigh potential passive gains. Freeing capital increases flexibility.

Skill alignment matters. Your first passive income stream should connect to strengths or interests. Alignment accelerates execution and reduces burnout.

A strong base allows automation to thrive. Without it, even promising income streams collapse under financial strain.

Digital Assets as Income Engines

Digital assets are among the most accessible forms of passive income in modern markets. Once created, they can be replicated infinitely at minimal cost. E-books, courses, templates, stock media, and subscription communities are scalable models.

The key to digital success is solving a problem clearly and specifically. Generic content struggles. Focused solutions thrive. When a digital product addresses a pressing need, demand sustains it.

Distribution platforms amplify reach. Marketplaces, email lists, social media funnels, and affiliate networks extend visibility. Automation tools manage delivery and payment processing.

Maintenance involves updates and marketing, but the income is not tied to daily production. This creates compounding opportunity.

Digital assets turn expertise into income streams. Knowledge becomes capital.

Investment-Based Passive Streams

Capital-based passive income leverages money rather than time. Dividend-paying stocks, index funds, bonds, real estate investment trusts (REITs), and rental properties produce recurring returns.

The power of investment-based income lies in compounding. Reinvested dividends accelerate growth. Time multiplies consistency.

Diversification protects stability. Multiple asset classes reduce volatility and smooth income streams.

Patience is essential. Market fluctuations are inevitable. Emotional discipline preserves long-term returns.

Investment streams require upfront capital, but they demand less operational oversight than business ventures. This makes them attractive for balanced portfolios.

Systemization and Automation

Automation transforms active effort into passive yield. Systems replace repetitive tasks. Software manages transactions. Processes standardize operations.

For example, subscription models automate recurring billing. Licensing agreements generate royalties. Affiliate marketing leverages other platforms' audiences.

Documentation is key. Clear processes allow delegation or automation. If you can outline the steps of a task, you can optimize it.

Technology reduces friction. Payment processors, content schedulers, analytics dashboards, and automation tools streamline workflows.

When systems operate efficiently, income flows with minimal intervention.

Scaling and Portfolio Balance

Passive income becomes powerful when diversified. Relying on a single stream introduces vulnerability. A balanced portfolio integrates digital, capital-based, and system-driven models.

Reinvest profits strategically. Early gains fuel additional streams. Momentum compounds.

Evaluate performance regularly. Identify underperforming streams and optimize or pivot. Continuous improvement sustains growth.

Risk management remains crucial. Avoid overconcentration in volatile sectors. Maintain liquidity.

A diversified passive portfolio transforms financial independence from theory into structure.

12 Passive Income Streams (Easy to Hard)

Easy to Obtain

1. High-Yield Savings Accounts
Low-risk accounts that generate modest interest on stored capital. Ideal for beginners building financial discipline.

2. Dividend-Paying Index Funds
Broad market funds that distribute dividends regularly. Accessible through brokerage accounts with minimal management.

3. Affiliate Marketing
Promoting products and earning commissions. Requires content creation but minimal product development.

4. Print-on-Demand Products
Design-based merchandise produced only when sold. No inventory management required.

Medium Difficulty

5. E-Books and Digital Guides

Requires content creation and marketing. High scalability once published.

6. Online Courses

Structured educational content delivered through platforms. Strong revenue potential with upfront effort.

7. Rental Property (Single Unit)

Generates monthly rent but requires capital and occasional oversight.

8. Subscription-Based Membership Communities

Recurring revenue from exclusive content or services. Needs consistent value delivery initially.

Hardest to Establish

9. Software or App Development
High upfront development costs but scalable with large potential user base.

10. Multi-Unit Real Estate Portfolio
Complex financing and management but strong long-term cash flow.

11. Intellectual Property Licensing
Royalties from patented inventions, creative works, or branded assets.

12. Automated E-Commerce Brand
Requires supply chain management, marketing systems, and optimization but scalable globally.

Exercises for Creating Passive Income

Exercise 1: Opportunity Mapping

Step 1: List all skills, hobbies, and knowledge areas.

Step 2: Identify which could be converted into digital assets.

Step 3: Research demand for each idea.

Step 4: Select one concept to develop within 60 days.

Step 5: Outline production and distribution steps.

Exercise 2: Capital Allocation Plan

Step 1: Determine available investment capital.

Step 2: Assess risk tolerance.

Step 3: Allocate funds across at least two asset classes.

Step 4: Automate monthly contributions.

Step 5: Review quarterly performance.

Exercise 3: Automation Blueprint

Step 1: Document a repetitive task in your workflow.

Step 2: Identify tools that could automate it.

Step 3: Implement automation software.

Step 4: Test and refine for efficiency.

Step 5: Measure time saved and reinvest it productively.

Journal Prompts

1. What does financial freedom mean to me?
2. Which passive income stream aligns with my strengths?
3. How much capital can I allocate safely?
4. What fears prevent me from starting?
5. How patient am I with long-term growth?
6. What digital asset could I create within 30 days?
7. How diversified is my income today?
8. What automation tools could improve efficiency?
9. What would change if my income continued while I slept?
10. What first step will I take this week?

Closing Reflection

Passive income is not magic. It is engineered leverage. It transforms effort into recurring reward. It shifts financial life from constant hustle to structured autonomy.

The path requires patience, discipline, and calculated risk. But once systems operate independently, freedom expands.

This chapter equips you with frameworks to begin building income streams that function beyond your daily labor. As these streams mature, they reinforce the millionaire foundation established earlier.

Income while sleeping is not fantasy. It is strategy executed consistently.

The next step is implementation.

Chapter 4: Scaling to Billionaire Status

Thinking in Systems, Not Salaries

Scaling to billionaire status begins with abandoning linear thinking. Salaries scale slowly. Systems scale exponentially. If income depends entirely on your direct effort, growth remains capped by time and energy. Billionaire-level scaling requires designing structures that operate independently of your daily presence.

A system is a repeatable process that produces consistent outcomes. It could be a sales funnel, a supply chain, a licensing model, a subscription ecosystem, or a digital distribution network. Systems multiply impact because they remove reliance on individual transactions and replace them with automated flows.

The shift from operator to architect is critical. Operators execute tasks. Architects design environments where value is produced continuously. The billionaire mindset focuses less on doing and more on designing. It asks: How can this be replicated? How can this be automated? How can this expand beyond me?

Scalable systems prioritize margin, not just revenue. High revenue with thin margins collapses under stress. Sustainable scaling demands operational efficiency. Cost control, predictable acquisition channels, and repeatable customer journeys strengthen expansion.

When you think in systems, you stop asking how to earn more hours and start asking how to multiply results without multiplying effort.

Leverage as a Force Multiplier

Leverage is the defining difference between millionaire growth and billionaire growth. There are four primary forms of leverage: capital, labor, code, and media. Billionaire-scale operations use multiple forms simultaneously.

Capital leverage means using money to generate more money. Strategic investments, acquisitions, and reinvestment cycles amplify returns. Instead of consuming profits, capital is deployed to accelerate growth.

Labor leverage involves building teams. Delegation frees time for strategic decisions. Billionaire-level scaling requires trust in specialists—operators, analysts, engineers, marketers—each amplifying productivity.

Code leverage refers to technology. Software scales infinitely without proportional cost increases. A digital product can serve one user or one million users with minimal additional expense.

Media leverage multiplies influence. Content, branding, and audience-building expand reach globally. Once authority is established, distribution becomes easier and more profitable.

When these forms of leverage intersect, growth accelerates dramatically.

Technology and Automation at Scale

Technology eliminates bottlenecks. Automation replaces repetitive tasks with intelligent workflows. Billionaire-level enterprises are built on automation infrastructure.

Customer relationship management systems track interactions. Automated email sequences nurture leads. Payment processors manage global transactions. Data analytics optimize conversion rates.

Automation also improves decision-making. Real-time dashboards provide insights into revenue, performance, and efficiency. Data-driven adjustments reduce guesswork and increase precision.

Cloud infrastructure allows global scalability without heavy physical investment. Digital delivery systems enable worldwide reach.

Technology transforms time into scalability. Once systems are configured, expansion requires less incremental effort.

Using AI as Strategic Leverage

Artificial intelligence is one of the most powerful scaling tools available today. AI enhances productivity, creativity, analysis, and operational efficiency. Used strategically, it becomes a multiplier.

AI can generate content drafts, analyze financial trends, automate customer support, optimize advertising campaigns, and personalize marketing at scale. This reduces operational costs and increases output.

AI-driven analytics identify patterns humans might miss. Predictive models forecast demand, optimize pricing, and refine targeting strategies. This creates competitive advantage.

In creative industries, AI accelerates ideation, research, editing, and design processes. It shortens production cycles while maintaining quality.

However, AI is not a replacement for strategy. It is a tool. Billionaire-level scaling occurs when human vision directs AI execution. The combination of strategic thinking and machine efficiency unlocks extraordinary leverage.

Time Mastery and Strategic Focus

Time becomes increasingly valuable as scale increases. Billionaire-level operators protect focus ruthlessly. They eliminate distractions and delegate low-impact tasks.

High-level scaling requires decision filtration. Not every opportunity deserves attention. Strategic alignment determines action. Focus remains on high-leverage activities.

Calendar discipline is essential. Blocks of uninterrupted thinking time drive innovation. Meetings are minimized and optimized.

Energy management complements time management. Physical health, mental clarity, and emotional resilience sustain long-term scaling efforts.

When time is allocated strategically, exponential growth becomes sustainable rather than overwhelming.

Global Expansion and Long-Term Vision

Scaling to billionaire status requires global perspective. Markets extend beyond borders. Digital infrastructure allows international reach without physical relocation.

Localization strategies adapt offerings to cultural and economic contexts. Partnerships accelerate entry into new regions.

Long-term vision guides expansion. Quarterly profits matter, but decades determine legacy. Billionaire-scale enterprises plan beyond immediate returns.

Brand equity compounds. Trust, reputation, and customer loyalty create durable advantage.

Scaling is not simply about bigger numbers. It is about building structures capable of sustained, global impact.

Exercises for Scaling

Exercise 1: Leverage Audit

Step 1: List all current income streams.

Step 2: Identify which rely entirely on your time.

Step 3: Determine how technology or delegation could reduce dependency.

Step 4: Implement one automation within 30 days.

Step 5: Track productivity improvement.

Exercise 2: AI Integration Plan

Step 1: Identify three tasks that consume significant time.

Step 2: Research AI tools capable of assisting with those tasks.

Step 3: Implement one AI tool into your workflow.

Step 4: Measure time saved over 30 days.

Step 5: Reinvest saved time into strategic growth planning.

Exercise 3: Scaling Blueprint Draft

Step 1: Define long-term revenue goals.

Step 2: Outline systems required to reach them.

Step 3: Identify key roles for delegation.

Step 4: Map automation tools to each system.

Step 5: Create a quarterly review schedule.

Journal Prompts

1. What does scaling truly mean to me?
2. Where am I trading time instead of building systems?
3. Which form of leverage am I underutilizing?
4. How can AI amplify my productivity?
5. What repetitive task can I eliminate this month?
6. What distractions limit strategic thinking?
7. How global is my current perspective?
8. What systems could expand beyond my direct involvement?
9. How comfortable am I delegating control?
10. What bold move would accelerate scaling dramatically?

Closing Reflection

Scaling to billionaire status is not about ambition alone. It is about structure, leverage, technology, and disciplined execution. Systems replace effort. Automation replaces repetition. AI enhances efficiency. Teams multiply output.

The transition from earning to scaling is transformative. It requires courage to relinquish control and confidence to trust systems.

Time becomes the most precious resource. Focus becomes the most valuable skill. Leverage becomes the most powerful tool.

Scaling is not accidental. It is engineered. With strategic thinking, intelligent automation, and disciplined execution, exponential growth becomes achievable.

The blueprint expands. The foundation strengthens. The horizon widens.

Now the challenge is not whether scaling is possible—but how boldly you will design it.

Chapter 5: Giving Back While Growing

Redefining Wealth Beyond Accumulation

True wealth is not measured solely by net worth. It is measured by impact. Accumulation without contribution creates imbalance. Growth that benefits only the individual is incomplete. Sustainable success integrates expansion with responsibility.

Many high achievers reach financial milestones only to discover that accumulation alone does not produce fulfillment. Purpose expands when wealth begins to serve something greater than personal comfort. Philanthropy transforms money from possession into influence.

Giving back does not require billionaire status. It begins with intention. Even modest contributions, when structured consistently, generate meaningful change. The habit of contribution scales alongside income.

Legacy is not built at the end of life. It is constructed through daily choices. Every investment, partnership, and charitable act contributes to a long-term narrative.

When wealth aligns with contribution, growth gains depth. Prosperity becomes multidimensional.

The Psychology of Generosity

Generosity strengthens abundance thinking. Scarcity clings. Abundance circulates. When you give strategically, you reinforce confidence in continued growth.

Philanthropy also builds identity. You begin to see yourself not only as a wealth builder but as a value distributor. This identity shapes decisions and expands influence.

Giving reduces fear of loss. It demonstrates trust in your ability to regenerate income. Confidence grows when you witness wealth flowing outward and returning through expanded networks and goodwill.

Research consistently shows that generosity increases life satisfaction. Contribution deepens meaning. Emotional wealth strengthens alongside financial wealth.

Generosity, when structured wisely, enhances both personal fulfillment and societal benefit.

Strategic Philanthropy

Effective giving is intentional. Emotional generosity is powerful, but strategic philanthropy multiplies impact. Identify causes aligned with your values and long-term vision.

Evaluate organizations for transparency, efficiency, and measurable outcomes. Donor-advised funds, private foundations, and direct community investment offer structured pathways.

Philanthropy can also integrate with business. Corporate social responsibility initiatives align profit with purpose. Sustainable practices, fair labor policies, and community reinvestment strengthen brand equity.

Legacy-driven giving considers generational impact. Scholarships, mentorship programs, and educational investments create long-term transformation.

Strategic philanthropy ensures that generosity produces measurable change rather than temporary relief.

Building Legacy Through Leadership

Legacy is not just financial. It is cultural. It is relational. It is ethical. Leadership decisions shape the environments you influence.

Mentorship accelerates legacy. Sharing knowledge creates exponential impact. When others succeed because of your guidance, your influence multiplies.

Ethical business practices establish trust. Reputation becomes a form of capital. Trust compounds over time and outlasts market fluctuations.

Documenting principles and systems ensures continuity. Succession planning protects enterprises beyond individual leadership.

A leader who integrates generosity into culture builds organizations that endure.

Balancing Growth and Contribution

Some fear that giving reduces growth potential. In reality, disciplined allocation enhances sustainability. Structured giving ensures balance.

Establish a contribution percentage tied to income growth. As revenue increases, so does impact. This creates alignment between prosperity and purpose.

Balance short-term giving with long-term investment. Immediate relief efforts coexist with long-term empowerment programs.

Financial discipline remains essential. Generosity should be intentional, not impulsive. Structure preserves sustainability.

When growth and giving coexist, wealth becomes resilient. Purpose stabilizes ambition.

Creating Intergenerational Impact

Legacy extends beyond a single lifetime. Intergenerational planning ensures that wealth serves future generations constructively.

Education is central. Teach financial literacy, ethical responsibility, and disciplined stewardship. Inherited wealth without preparation dissolves quickly.

Establish trusts or structured vehicles that protect assets while funding meaningful causes. Long-term frameworks preserve both capital and mission.

Encourage entrepreneurial thinking in younger generations. Empower them to build rather than depend.

When legacy planning integrates values, structure, and education, wealth becomes a lasting force for progress.

Exercises for Building Legacy

Exercise 1: Values Clarification

Step 1: List core values that define your vision of success.

Step 2: Identify causes aligned with those values.

Step 3: Research three organizations or initiatives.

Step 4: Choose one to support consistently.

Step 5: Evaluate impact annually.

Exercise 2: Contribution Allocation Plan

Step 1: Determine a percentage of income for philanthropy.

Step 2: Automate contributions monthly.

Step 3: Divide allocations between immediate aid and long-term initiatives.

Step 4: Track total annual giving.

Step 5: Adjust percentage as income grows.

Exercise 3: Legacy Blueprint Draft

Step 1: Define the impact you want to leave behind.

Step 2: Outline mentorship or educational initiatives you can begin now.

Step 3: Draft basic succession or estate planning goals.

Step 4: Document personal principles for future generations.

Step 5: Review and refine annually.

Journal Prompts

1. What does legacy mean to me personally?
2. How do I want to be remembered beyond wealth?
3. Which causes resonate deeply with my values?
4. What fears arise when I consider giving more?
5. How can philanthropy align with my business growth?
6. Who has influenced my life through generosity?
7. What knowledge can I share to accelerate others' growth?
8. How disciplined is my current giving structure?
9. What long-term impact would fulfill me most?
10. What first step can I take this month toward building legacy?

Closing Reflection

Wealth without contribution is incomplete. Growth without purpose is fragile. Giving back strengthens both the giver and the receiver.

Legacy is built through consistent, intentional acts of generosity and leadership. It reflects values embedded into systems, families, businesses, and communities.

As you scale income and expand influence, remember that the greatest measure of success is impact. Money multiplies options. Purpose multiplies meaning.

Giving while growing ensures that prosperity transcends personal gain. It transforms wealth into enduring influence.

The blueprint concludes not with accumulation—but with contribution.

Appendix A: Practical Tools for Financial Growth

This appendix serves as your operational toolkit. Strategy without structure fades. Motivation without systems dissolves. Financial growth becomes sustainable when supported by practical tools that convert intention into execution. The following frameworks, templates, and implementation guides are designed to help you move from theory to measurable results.

1. The Financial Snapshot Template

Purpose: Establish complete financial clarity within 60 minutes.

Income Inventory

- Primary income source
- Secondary income sources
- Irregular income
- Investment income
- Total monthly gross income
- Total monthly net income

Expense Breakdown

- Housing
- Utilities
- Food
- Insurance
- Transportation
- Debt payments
- Subscriptions
- Discretionary spending
- Miscellaneous
- Total monthly expenses

Net Worth Formula

Assets – Liabilities = Net Worth

Repeat this snapshot monthly. Track trends. Growth begins with measurement.

2. The 50–30–20 (Modified Growth) Allocation Model

Traditional budgeting models focus on stability. This version integrates aggressive growth.

- **50% Stability Layer** – Essentials and fixed expenses
- **20% Growth Layer** – Investments, business reinvestment, skill development
- **10% Reserve Layer** – Emergency savings
- **10% Opportunity Layer** – Strategic risk capital
- **10% Lifestyle Layer** – Enjoyment without guilt

Adjust percentages based on income level, but always maintain a Growth Layer. Without it, expansion stalls.

3. Net Worth Tracking System

Create a monthly spreadsheet with the following columns:

- Date
- Cash & Savings
- Investments
- Business Equity
- Property Value
- Total Assets
- Total Liabilities
- Net Worth
- Monthly Change
- Year-to-Date Growth

Visual tracking reinforces progress psychology. Even small improvements compound.

4. Income Stream Diversification Map

Use this grid to categorize your income sources:

Type	Active	Semi-Passive	Passive
Employment	✓		
Freelance	✓		
Digital Products		✓	
Dividends			✓
Rental Income		✓	✓

Goal: Move progressively from active to passive categories.

5. Skill Capital Growth Framework

Step 1: Identify high-income skills aligned with your interests.

Step 2: Rank them by market demand.

Step 3: Choose one skill to master per quarter.

Step 4: Allocate weekly learning time.

Step 5: Monetize skill within 90 days.

Skill development often produces the highest ROI in early wealth stages.

6. Investment Allocation Blueprint

Conservative Allocation Example

- 40% Broad Market Index Funds
- 20% Dividend Stocks
- 20% Bonds or Fixed Income
- 10% Real Estate (REITs)
- 10% Cash Reserve

Growth-Oriented Allocation Example

- 60% Equity Index Funds
- 20% Real Estate
- 10% Alternative Assets
- 10% Cash

Always adjust based on risk tolerance and time horizon.

7. The Compounding Calculator Formula

Compound Growth Formula:

Future Value = Principal × (1 + Rate)^Time

Example:

$10,000 invested at 8% annually for 20 years:

10,000 × (1.08)^20 ≈ $46,609

Consistency beats intensity. Time amplifies discipline.

8. Opportunity Evaluation Checklist

Before investing time or money, ask:

- Does this align with long-term goals?
- What is the expected ROI?
- What is the worst-case scenario?
- Can this scale?
- Is there leverage involved?
- Does this diversify or concentrate risk?
- What expertise do I need?
- What is the exit strategy?

Avoid emotional investments. Use structured evaluation.

9. AI Productivity Integration Guide

Artificial Intelligence can accelerate growth when used strategically.

Use AI For:

- Drafting business plans
- Financial forecasting models
- Market research summaries
- Content production acceleration
- Automation scripting
- Customer data analysis
- Lead scoring optimization
- Investment research assistance

AI Workflow Example

1. Define objective.
2. Use AI to gather structured insights.
3. Validate data with independent research.
4. Implement action.
5. Measure results.

AI enhances execution speed, not decision authority. Strategic oversight remains essential.

10. Weekly CEO Review Framework
Set aside 60–90 minutes weekly.

Review:

- Revenue performance
- Expense control
- Investment growth
- Skill development progress
- New opportunities
- Risk exposure
- Automation efficiency
- AI optimization usage

Plan:

- Top 3 strategic priorities
- Delegation tasks
- Capital allocation decisions

Consistency transforms review into growth acceleration.

11. Emergency Fund Acceleration Plan

Step 1: Calculate 6 months of essential expenses.

Step 2: Divide by target timeframe (e.g., 12 months).

Step 3: Automate monthly transfers.

Step 4: Deposit bonuses or windfalls directly.

Step 5: Protect fund—do not invest aggressively.

Stability increases risk tolerance for higher-return opportunities.

12. Long-Term Wealth Dashboard Metrics
Track these annually:

- Net Worth Growth Rate
- Passive Income Ratio
- Debt-to-Asset Ratio
- Savings Rate
- Investment Return %
- Business Margin %
- AI Efficiency Gains
- Philanthropic Contribution %

Metrics transform ambition into measurable progress.

Implementation Roadmap

Month 1

- Complete financial snapshot.
- Begin net worth tracking.
- Establish growth allocation.

Month 2–3

- Launch first passive income stream.
- Begin skill upgrade cycle.
- Automate at least one financial system.

Month 4–6

- Diversify investments.
- Implement AI productivity tools.
- Conduct quarterly strategic review.

Year 1

- Increase passive income percentage.
- Optimize systems.
- Reinvest profits into scalable assets.

Final Integration Principles

1. Clarity precedes growth.
2. Systems outperform effort.
3. Skills multiply income.
4. Automation multiplies time.
5. AI multiplies execution speed.
6. Diversification protects expansion.
7. Consistency compounds results.

Financial growth is not mystical. It is mechanical. When practical tools support disciplined action, results accelerate.

This appendix is not meant to be read once—it is meant to be used repeatedly. Return to it. Update it. Refine it. Implement it.

The blueprint becomes reality when tools meet execution.

Closing Reflection

Appendix A is not a conclusion — it is a control panel.

Everything in this book becomes powerful only when implemented. The tools provided here are not theoretical exercises; they are operational mechanisms. Financial growth is not driven by inspiration alone. It is driven by systems, repetition, measurement, and refinement.

You now possess frameworks for clarity, allocation, diversification, automation, AI leverage, and long-term tracking. These tools remove ambiguity. They replace emotional decision-making with structured action. When you measure consistently, you improve consistently. When you automate intelligently, you scale sustainably. When you review strategically, you adjust before mistakes compound.

Financial independence is not built through occasional effort. It is engineered through disciplined cycles of action and evaluation. The snapshot becomes a monthly ritual. The net worth tracker becomes a scoreboard. The AI integration plan becomes an efficiency multiplier. The opportunity checklist becomes a filter for focus.

Return to these tools often. Update them. Refine them. Expand them as your income grows and your influence widens.

The blueprint has been laid out. The mindset has been built. The systems have been designed.

Now execution determines everything.

Your financial future is no longer abstract. It is measurable, actionable, and within your control.

Message from the Author:

I hope you enjoyed this book, I love astrology and knew there was not a book such as this out on the shelf. I love metaphysical items as well. Please check out my other books:

-Life of Government Benefits

-My life of Hell

-My life with Hydrocephalus

-Red Sky

-World Domination:Woman's rule

-World Domination:Woman's Rule 2: The War

-Life and Banishment of Apophis: book 1

-The Kidney Friendly Diet

-The Ultimate Hemp Cookbook

-Creating a Dispensary(legally)

-Cleanliness throughout life: the importance of showering from childhood to adulthood.

-Strong Roots: The Risks of Overcoddling children

-Hemp Horoscopes: Cosmic Insights and Earthly Healing

- Celestial Hemp Navigating the Zodiac: Through the Green Cosmos

-Astrological Hemp: Aligning The Stars with Earth's Ancient Herb

-The Astrological Guide to Hemp: Stars, Signs, and Sacred Leaves

-Green Growth: Innovative Marketing Strategies for your Hemp Products and Dispensary

-Cosmic Cannabis

-Astrological Munchies

-Henry The Hemp

-Zodiacal Roots: The Astrological Soul Of Hemp

- **Green Constellations: Intersection of Hemp and Zodiac**

-Hemp in The Houses: An astrological Adventure Through The Cannabis Galaxy

-Galactic Ganja Guide

Heavenly Hemp

Zodiac Leaves

Doctor Who Astrology

Cannastrology

Stellar Satvias and Cosmic Indicas

Celestial Cannabis: A Zodiac Journey

AstroHerbology: The Sky and The Soil: Volume 1

AstroHerbology:Celestial Cannabis:Volume 2

Cosmic Cannabis Cultivation

The Starry Guide to Herbal Harmony: Volume 1

The Starry Guide to Herbal Harmony: Cannabis Universe: Volume 2

Yugioh Astrology: Astrological Guide to Deck, Duels and more

Nightmare Mansion: Echoes of The Abyss

Nightmare Mansion 2: Legacy of Shadows

Nightmare Mansion 3: Shadows of the Forgotten

Nightmare Mansion 4: Echoes of the Damned

The Life and Banishment of Apophis: Book 2

Nightmare Mansion: Halls of Despair

Healing with Herb: Cannabis and Hydrocephalus

Planetary Pot: Aligning with Astrological Herbs: Volume 1

Fast Track to Freedom: 30 Days to Financial Independence Using AI, Assets, and Agile Hustles

Cosmic Hemp Pathways

How to Become Financially Free in 30 Days: 10,000 Paths to Prosperity

Zodiacal Herbage: Astrological Insights: Volume 1

Nightmare Mansion: Whispers in the Walls

The Daleks Invade Atlantis

Henry the hemp and Hydrocephalus

10X The Kidney Friendly Diet

Cannabis Universe: Adult coloring book

Hemp Astrology: The Healing Power of the Stars

Zodiacal Herbage: Astrological Insights: Cannabis Universe: Volume 2

Planetary Pot: Aligning with Astrological Herbs: Cannabis Universes: Volume 2

Doctor Who: Convergence Protocol – The Replicator War

Nightmare Mansion: Curse of the Blood Moon

The Celestial Stoner: A Guide to the Zodiac

Cosmic Pleasures: Sex Toy Astrology for Every Sign

Hydrocephalus Astrology: Navigating the Stars and Healing Waters

Lapis and the Mischievous Chocolate Bar

Celestial Positions: Sexual Astrology for Every Sign

Apophis's Shadow Work Journal: : A Journey of Self-Discovery and Healing

Kinky Cosmos: Sexual Kink Astrology for Every Sign

Digital Cosmos: The Astrological Digimon Compendium

Stellar Seeds: The Cosmic Guide to Growing with Astrology

Apophis's Daily Gratitude Journal

Cat Astrology: Feline Mysteries of the Cosmos

The Cosmic Kama Sutra: An Astrological Guide to Sexual Positions

Unleash Your Potential: A Guided Journal Powered by AI Insights

Whispers of the Enchanted Grove

Cosmic Pleasures: An Astrological Guide to Sexual Kinks

369, 12 Manifestation Journal

Whisper of the nocturne journal(blank journal for writing or drawing)

The Boogey Book

Locked In Reflection: A Chastity Journey Through Locktober

Generating Wealth Quickly:How to Generate $100,000 in 24 Hours

Star Magic: Harness the Power of the Universe

The Flatulence Chronicles: A Fart Journal for Self-Discovery

The Doctor and The Death Moth

Seize the Day: A Personal Seizure Tracking Journal

The Ultimate Boogeyman Safari: A Journey into the Boogie World and Beyond

Whispers of Samhain: 1,000 Spells of Love, Luck, and Lunar Magic: Samhain Spell Book

Apophis's guides:Witch's Spellbook Crafting Guide for Halloween

Frost & Flame: The Enchanted Yule Grimoire of 1000 Winter Spells

The Ultimate Boogey Goo Guide & Spooky Activities for Halloween Fun

Harmony of the Scales: A Libra's Spellcraft for Balance and Beauty

The Enchanted Advent: 36 Days of Christmas Wonders

Nightmare Mansion: The Labyrinth of Screams

Harvest of Enchantment: 1,000 Spells of Gratitude, Love, and Fortune for Thanksgiving

The Boogey Chronicles: A Journal of Nightly Encounters and Shadowy Secrets

The 12 Days of Financial Freedom: A Step-by-Step Christmas Countdown to Transform Your Finances

Sigil of the Eternal Spiral Blank Journal

A Christmas Feast: Timeless Recipes for Every Meal

Holiday Stress-Free Solutions: A Survival Guide to Thriving During the Festive Season

Yu-Gi-Oh! Holiday Gifting Mastery: The Ultimate Guide for Fans and Newcomers Alike

Holiday Harmony: A Hydrocephalus Survival Guide for the Festive Season

Celestial Craft: The Witch's Almanac for 2025 – A Cosmic Guide to Manifestations, Moons, and Mystical Events

Doctor Who: The Toymaker's Winter Wonderland

Tulsa King Unveiled: A Thrilling Guide to Stallone's Mafia Masterpiece

Pendulum Craft: A Complete Guide to Crafting and Using Personalized Divination Tools

Nightmare Mansion: Santa's Eternal Eve

Starlight Noel: A Cosmic Journey through Christmas Mysteries

The Dark Architect: Unlocking the Blueprint of Existence

Surviving the Embrace: The Ultimate Guide to Encounters with The Hugging Molly

The Enchanted Codex: Secrets of the Craft for Witches, Wiccans, and Pagans

Harvest of Gratitude: A Complete Thanksgiving Guide

Yuletide Essentials: A Complete Guide to an Authentic and Magical Christmas

Celestial Smokes: A Cosmic Guide to Cigars and Astrology

Living in Balance: A Comprehensive Survival Guide to Thriving with Diabetes Insipidus

Cosmic Symbiosis: The Venom Zodiac Chronicles

The Cursed Paw of Ambition

Cosmic Symbiosis: The Astrological Venom Journal

Celestial Wonders Unfold: A Stargazer's Guide to the Cosmos (2024-2029)

The Ultimate Black Friday Prepper's Guide: Mastering Shopping Strategies and Savings

Cosmic Sales: The Astrological Guide to Black Friday Shopping

Legends of the Corn Mother and Other Harvest Myths

Whispers of the Harvest: The Corn Mother's Journal

The Evergreen Spellbook

The Doctor Meets the Boogeyman

The White Witch of Rose Hall's SpellBook

The Gingerbread Golem's Shadow: A Study in Sweet Darkness

The Gingerbread Golem Codex: An Academic Exploration of Sweet Myths

The Gingerbread Golem Grimoire: Sweet Magicks and Spells for the Festive Witch

The Curse of the Gingerbread Golem

10-minute Christmas Crafts for kids

Christmas Crisis Solutions: The Ultimate Last-Minute Survival Guide

Gingerbread Golem Recipes: Holiday Treats with a Magical Twist

The Infinite Key: Unlocking Mystical Secrets of the Ages

Enchanted Yule: A Wiccan and Pagan Guide to a Magical and Memorable Season

Dinosaurs of Power: Unlocking Ancient Magick

Astro-Dinos: The Cosmic Guide to Prehistoric Wisdom

Gallifrey's Yule Logs: A Festive Doctor Who Cookbook

The Dino Grimoire: Secrets of Prehistoric Magick

The Gift They Never Knew They Needed

The Gingerbread Golem's Culinary Alchemy: Enchanting Recipes for a Sweetly Dark Feast

A Time Lord Christmas: Holiday Adventures with the Doctor

Krampusproofing Your Home: Defensive Strategies for Yule

Silent Frights: A Collection of Christmas Creepypastas to Chill Your Bones

Santa Raptor's Jolly Carnage: A Dino-Claus Christmas Tale

Prehistoric Palettes: A Dino Wicca Coloring Journey

The Christmas Wishkeeper Chronicles

The Starlight Sleigh: A Holiday Journey

Elf Secrets: The True Magic of the North Pole

Candy Cane Conjurations

Cooking with Kids: Recipes Under 20 Minutes

Doctor Who: The TARDIS Confiscation

The Anxiety First Aid Kit: Quick Tools to Calm Your Mind

Frosty Whispers: A Winter's Tale

The Infinite Key: Unlocking the Secrets to Prosperity, Resilience, and Purpose

The Grasping Void: Why You'll Regret This Purchase

Astrology for Busy Bees: Star Signs Simplified

The Instant Focus Formula: Cut Through the Noise

The Secret Language of Colors: Unlocking the Emotional Codes

Sacred Fossil Chronicles: Blank Journal

The Christmas Cottage Miracle

Feeding Frenzy: Graboid-Inspired Recipes

Manifest in Minutes: The Quick Law of Attraction Guide

The Symbiote Chronicles: Doctor Who's Venomous Journey

Think Tiny, Grow Big: The Minimalist Mindset

The Energy Key: Unlocking Limitless Motivation

New Year, New Magic: Manifesting Your Best Year Yet

Unstoppable You: Mastering Confidence in Minutes

Infinite Energy: The Secret to Never Feeling Drained

Lightning Focus: Mastering the Art of Productivity in a Distracted World

Saturnalia Manifestation Magick: A Guide to Unlocking Abundance During the Solstice

Graboids and Garland: The Ultimate Tremors-Themed Christmas Guide

12 Nights of Holiday Magic

The Power of Pause: 60-Second Mindfulness Practices

The Quick Reset: How to Reclaim Your Life After Burnout

The Shadow Eater: A Tale of Despair and Survival

The Micro-Mastery Method: Transform Your Skills in Just Minutes a Day

Reclaiming Time: How to Live More by Doing Less

Chronovore: The Eternal Nexus

The Mind Reset: Unlocking Your Inner Peace in a Chaotic World

Confidence Code: Building Unshakable Self-Belief

Baby the Vampire Terrier

Baby the Vampire Terrier's Christmas Adventure

Celestial Streams: The Content Creator's Astrology Manual

The Wealth Whisperer: Unlocking Abundance with Everyday Actions

The Energy Equation: Maximize Your Output Without Burning Out

The Happiness Algorithm: Science-Backed Steps to Joyful Living

Stress-Free Success: Achieving Goals Without Anxiety

Mindful Wealth: The New Blueprint for Financial Freedom

The Festive Flavors of New Year: A Culinary Celebration

The Master's Gambit: Keys of Eternal Power

Shadowed Secrets: Groundhog Day Mysteries

Beneath the Burrow: Lessons from the Groundhog

Spring's Whispers: The Groundhog's Prediction

The Limitless Mindset: Unlock Your Untapped Potential

The Focus Funnel: How to Cut Through Chaos and Get Results

Bold Moves: Building Courage to Live on Your Terms

The Daily Shift: Simple Practices for Lasting Transformation

The Quarter-Life Reset: Thriving in Your 20s and 30s

The Art of Shadowplay: Building Your Own Personal Myth

The Eternal Loop: Finding Purpose in Repetition

Burrowing Wisdom: Life Lessons from the Groundhog

Shadow Work: A Groundhog Day Perspective

Love in Bloom: 5-Minute Romantic Gestures

The Shadowspell Codex: Secrets of Forbidden Magick

The Burnout Cure: Finding Balance in a Busy World

The Groundhog Prophecy: Unlocking Seasonal Secrets

Nog Tales: The Spirited History of Eggnog

Six More Weeks: Embracing Seasonal Transitions

The Lumivian Chronicles: Fragments of the Fifth Dimension

Money on Your Mind: A Beginner's Guide to Wealth

The Focus Fix: Breaking Through Distraction

January's Spirit Keepers: Mystical Protectors of the Cold
Creativity Unchained: Unlocking Your Wildest Ideas in 2025
Manifestation Mastery: 365 Days to Rewrite Your Reality
The Groundhog's Mirror: Reflecting on Change
The Weeping Angels' Christmas Curse
Burrowed in Time: A Groundhog Day Journey
Heartbeats: Poems to Share with Your Valentine
Dino Wicca: The Sacred Grimoire of Prehistoric Magick
Courage of the Pride: Finding Your Inner Roar
The Lion's Leap: Bold Moves for Big Results
Healthy Hustle: Achieving Without Overworking
Practical Manifesting: Turning Dreams into Reality in 2025
Jurassic Pharaohs: Unlocking the Magick of Ancient Egypt and Dino Wicca
The Happiness Equation: Small Changes for Big Joy
The Confidence Compass: Finding Your Inner Strength
Whispers in the Hollow: Tales of the Forgotten Beasts
Echoes from the Hollow: The Return of Forgotten Beasts
The Hollow Ascendant: The Rise of the Forgotten Beasts
The Relationship Reset: Building Better Connections
Mastering the Morning: How to Win the Day Before 8 AM
The Shadow's Dance: Groundhog Day Symbolism
Cupid's Kitchen: Quick Valentine's Day Recipes
Valentine's Day on a Budget: Love Without Breaking the Bank
Astrocraft: Aligning the Stars in the World of Minecraft
Forecasting Life: Groundhog Day Reflections

Bleeding Hearts: Twisted Tales of Valentine's Terror

Herbal Smoke Revolution: The Ultimate Guide to Nature's Cigarette Alternative

Winter's Wrath: The Complete Survival Blueprint for Extreme Freezes.

The Groundhog's Shadow: A Tale of Seasons
Burrowed Insights: Wisdom from the Groundhog

Sensual Strings: The Art of Erotic Bondage
Whispered Flames: Unlocking the Power of Fire Play
Forgotten Shadows: A Guide to Cryptids Lost to Time
Six Weeks of Secrets: Groundhog Day's Hidden Messages
Shadows and Cycles: Groundhog Day Reflections
The Art of Love Letters: Crafting the Perfect Message
Romantic Getaways at Home: Turning Your Space into Paradise
Purrfect Brews: A Cat Lover's Guide to Coffee and Companionship
The Groundhog's Wisdom: Timeless Lessons for Modern Life
The Shadow Oracle: Groundhog Day as a Predictor
Emerging from the Burrow: A Journey of Renewal
The Language of Love: Learning Your Partner's Love Style
Authorpreneur: The Ultimate Blueprint for Writing, Publishing, and Thriving as an Author
Weathering the Seasons: Groundhog Day Perspectives
Valentine's Day Magic: A Guide to Romantic Rituals
The Shadow Chronicles: Stories of Groundhog Day
Love and Laughter: Fun Games for Valentine's Day
AstroRealty: Unlocking the Stars for Property Success
The Groundhog's Path: A Guide to Seasonal Balance
Groundhog Day Diaries: Reflections in the Shadow
The Groundhog's Light: Illuminating the Path Ahead
Valentine's Traditions from Around the World
AI Wealth Revolution: Unlocking the Trillionaire Mindset
Love Rekindled: Reigniting Passion in Relationships
Single and Thriving: Self-Love on Valentine's Day
Emerald Legends: Mystical Tales of Ireland
Green Alchemy: Harnessing Nature's Magic
The Hearts of Horror: A Valentine's Day Nightmare
The Leprechaun's Guide to Wealth and Wisdom
Dancing with the Sidhe: Celebrating the Otherworld

Shamrocks and Shadows: Mysteries of the Green Isle

Emerald Energy: Harnessing Luck and Growth

The Gingerbread Golem's Valentine: A Sweetheart's Guide to Love and Enchantment

The Celtic Knot: Weaving Life and Destiny

Green Fire: Elemental Magic for St. Patrick's Day

Clover Chronicles: Finding Your Inner Luck

Ireland's Mystical Creatures: A Field Guide

Gingerbread Golem's Love Almanac

Prowl and Thrive: The Lion's Guide to Success

Love Alchemy: Transforming Your Life Through Heart Energy

WORLD DOMINATION: Woman's Rule 3:The New Life

The Midnight Rose: A Guide to Lunar Love Spells

The Forbidden Letters: Writing Your Own Love Prophecy

Luck and Lore: St. Patrick's Day for Modern Mystics

The Green Path: A Pagan Celebration of Renewal

The Dark Architect's Guide to Reprogramming Reality

Prankster's Paradise: A Guide to Harmless Hijinks

Manifest Your Reality: The Law of Attraction Simplified

The TARDIS Owner's Manual: Understanding the Doctor's Ship: *A complete guide to the TARDIS, its technology, secrets, and mysteries*

Starlit Romance: Astrology Secrets for Finding True Love

The Time Lord's Atlas: A Complete Guide to the Whoniverse: ***A breakdown of the locations, planets, and dimensions explored in Doctor Who***

Sweetheart Shadows: The Dark Side of Love and Attraction

February Fire: Reigniting Passion in Every Area of Life

The Self-Love Toolkit: 5 Ways to Embrace Who You Are

February Sparks: Ignite Your Dreams in 28 Days

March to Success: A 31-Day Action Blueprint

Ancient Paths: The 13 Sacred Principles of Dino Wicca

Echoes of Tomorrow: Navigating the AI Revolution
The Wellness Blueprint: Balancing Mind, Body, and Soul
Green Horizons: Sustainable Living for a Better Tomorrow
The AI Wealth Code: How to Make Millions with Automation
AI-Powered Creativity: Writing, Art, and Music for Profit
Extinction Rites: Rebirthing Your Soul Through Prehistoric Magick
Sacred Serpents tarot
Celestial Enchantment blank journal
Star Strains
Culinary Journeys: Exploring Global Flavors at Home
The Hollowvale Curse
The Hollowvale Harvest
The Egg of Transformation: Awakening Your Inner Power
Blooming Into Power: A Wiccan Guide to Spring Awakening
The Nightmare Nexus: The Third Doctor's Perilous Haunting
Digital Detox: Reclaiming Your Life in a Connected World
Ostara's Path: Walking the Spiral of Renewal
The Sacred Hare
Financial Freedom: Building Wealth in the Modern Age
Spring's Cauldron: Stirring the Waters of Change
The Hollowvale Pact
Quantum Consciousness: The Science of Reality Shifting
The Hollowvale Hunger
The Sacred Waters Within: A Witch's Guide to Hydrocephalus Magick
The Raven's Nest: Building a Life of Unshakable Stability
AI and the Human Mind: The Future of Intelligence
The Hollowvale Reckoning
Timeless Love: Building and Maintaining Lasting Relationships
The Raven's Roar: Unlocking Unstoppable Confidence
Raven Sight: Awakening Intuition and Inner Wisdom

The Butterfly Effect: Small Changes, Big Transformations
Taming the Boogeyman: How to Conquer Your Inner Fears
The Magick of Green: Awakening Earth's Energy in You
The Entrepreneurial Mindset: Secrets to Business Success
The Hollowvale End
The Shadow Luck Ritual: Reclaiming Power from Your Dark Side
Spring Magick for Beginners: A Simple Guide to Seasonal Energy Work
Doctor Who: The Hollowvale Conundrum
The March of Miracles: Unlocking Synchronicities in Spring
Unveiling the Cosmos: A Guide to Stargazing and Space Exploration
The Ultimate Guide to Surviving an Economic Collapse
The AI Gold Rush: How to Profit from the AI Revolution
Bastet's Shadow: The Hidden Power of Feline Magick
The Bastet Codex: Unlocking the Goddess's Magickal Secrets
Purring Spells: Harnessing Bastet's Healing Frequencies
Bastet's Nine Lives: Rebirth, Transformation, and Immortality Spells
Primal Currents: Hydrocephalus Magick in the Path of Dino Wicca
The Digital Gold Rush: Mastering E-Commerce and Online Sales
Future Shock: Adapting to the Next Decade of Change
The Quantum Mindset: Think Like a Billionaire
Sacred Motherhood: Awakening the Divine Feminine Within
The Mother's Spellbook: Enchantments for Love, Protection, and Prosperity
The Witch's Guide to Parenting: Raising Empowered and Intuitive Children
The Magick of Motherhood: Reclaiming Your Power Through Rituals

The Pagan Path to Self-Love: A Goddess's Guide to Worth and Confidence
Wild Woman Magick: Unleashing Your Primal Power
The Money Magnet Blueprint: Unlocking Unlimited Wealth
Biohacking 101: Unlock Your Body's Full Potential
The Wild Father: A Pagan Guide to Strength and Wisdom
The Sacred Masculine: Unlocking Your Inner Power
The Druid's Compass
The Warrior's Mindset
The Father's Fire
Odin's Path
Ancestral Bonds
The House That Whispers
The Magician's Code
The Wild Hunt
The Green Man's Path
The Altar of Success
The Shadow and the Sword
The High Priestess's Guide to Energy Healing
The Lunar Mother
The Sacred Self-Care Grimoire
The Womb Wisdom Codex
The Wheel of the Mother
The Witch's Guide to Manifestation
The Q2 Reset
The Ultimate Guide to AI-Powered Passive Income
Escape the 9-5
AI Feline Fortunes
The Tear-Stained Grimoire
Razorblade Runes
Cemetery Sirens
The Midnight Wristwatch
The Town That Forgets

AI Horror & Creepypasta
The Hollow Frequency
The Breach Echo
The Quiet Between Worlds
The Sigil of Tharan-Khul
Summon the Vault of Y'ha'ten
The Becoming Codex
The Profit of Az'ra-nar
The Drowned Logos
Echoes of the Eldritch Will
The Deep Ledger
Necronomicon of Networth
Covenant of the Wealthwyrm
The Whisperer's Manifesto
The Rites of Azh-K'luth
The Ark of the Crawling Coin
The Tithe of Shadows
Inkheart Abyss
The Timewinds of Y'ha-nthlei
The Spiral Labyrinth of Azag-Nirrh
The Gallifreyan Heresy of the Black Pharaoh
The Psalms of Nyog-Sotha
Black Rain Alchemy
The Infinite Maw
The Entropic Blueprint
The Oracle of Sh'guul
The Book of Breach
The Drowned Saint's Testament
Dreamcraft of the Sleeper God
The Silence Market
Cthonomics: The Dark Wealth Algorithm
Invocation of the Ten-Eyed King
Wealthbound to the Wyrm Below

Become the Unnameable
Codex of the Sovereign Flame
Rituals of Relentless Becoming
The Shadow Ascends
The Eyes Beneath You
The Will That Wakes Worlds
Silence Is a Weapon
The Mirror That Screams
The Whisper Between Moments
The Mind That Devours Fear
The Myth of the Finished Self
The Architect of Your Madness
The Voice You've Buried
The Discipline of Madness
Stormborn: Awakening Your Inner Tempest
The Mind That Ate Time
Unbind Your Becoming
The Pact You Owe Yourself
The Devourer's Diet
The Acid That Carves the Path
The Tower You Must Burn
The Breath Between Worlds
Speak Like the Deep
The Labyrinth Within
The Spine of the Sea God
Rejection Is a Portal
The Crown You Refused
The Scar Is the Spell
The Lightless Flame
The Habit of Becoming Horrific
ChickenJockey Chaos
The Gatekeeper Within
You Are Not Your Name

The Compass of the Mad
The Archive of Unsent Letters
What the Mirror Can't Show You
The Knife You Needed
Worship Nothing, Become Everything
The Other Voice
The Body the World Forgot
The Vein of the Void
The Black Bone Codex
The Puzzle of the Hidden Self (Millennium Puzzle)
The Eye That Sees the Lie *(Millennium Eye)*
The Ring of Return (Millennium Ring)
The Rod of Relentless Will ***(Millennium Rod)***
The Tally of the Soul (Millennium Tauk/Necklace)
The Key to the Locked Timeline (Millennium Key)
The Scale of Sacred Decisions (Millennium Scales)
Inferno Bites: The UnOfficial Minecraft Lava Cookbook
Rot in the Attic
Prana: The Hidden Force of Your Infinite Self
The Shadow Realm Within: Transforming Darkness Into Destiny
The Borderland Collapse
Claws of Protection: Bastet's Defensive Magick
Mr. Ring-a-Ding's Madness
Yugioh Astrology: Celestial Deckcraft and Duel Destiny (2026–2027 Edition)
The Seal You Signed: Unlocking the Power You Once Feared
The Puzzle of Infinite Minds: Unlocking the Mentalism Hidden Within
The Eye That Mirrors the All: Secrets of Inner Reflection
Doctor Who: The Toymaker's Broadcast
The Rod of Eternal Flow: Commanding the Currents of Vibration

Golden Eyes of Bastet: Enhancing Psychic Vision
The Key of Dual Forces: Balance Within the Polarity
The Scales of Living Rhythm: Timing the Dance of Life
The Necklace of Hidden Cause: Weaving the Webs of Fate
The Ring of Secret Masters: Rising Through the All Within All
Daggers of the Dying Deep
Bastet's Wealth and Fortune Magick: Prosperity Rituals of the Goddess
The Tide that Speaks
The Scrolls of Petosiris: 13 Rituals from the Feathered Eye
Petosiris and the Living Plague of Osirion
Feline Fire: Bastet's Passion and Love Magick
The Star Altar of Petosiris
Bastet's Whiskers: Supernatural Sensory Magick
The Bastet Grimoire
Feeding the Shadows
The Mouthless Prayer
The Spiral Wound
Becoming the Ibis: Lessons from Petosiris's Mind
The Crimson Coven: Cola Magick for Sweet Dominion
Sacred Cat's Paw
The Soda Zodiac: A Flavor for Every Sign
Covenant of the Crawling Flame
The Ink of Ish'Zur
Frothroot: The Thirst That Ate the World
The Golden Glyphs of Prosperity
The Etherbind Codex
Echoes of the Resistance: Reclaiming the You That Survived
Harnessed Minds: Breaking Free from Mental Control
The Eyes in the Smoke
Rootwake: The Carbon Covenant
Skitter Logic: Unlearning the Fear That Built You

Doctor Who: The World That Froths
Rootwake: The Fizz That Rewrites Flesh
Rootwake: Frothfather of the World
The Holly Pact: Blood Beneath the Mistletoe
The 2nd Mass Principle: Building Unbreakable Tribes
Web of Wits: A Survival Guide to Encounters with Anasi the Spider (Aunt Nancy)
The Hexbreaking Handbook: Effective Spells to Remove Curses
Pop Alchemy: Transform Your Life One Sip at a Time
The Mason Code: Leading in Unleadable Times
Petosiris and the Fifth Chamber of Thoth
The Ether Seed Within
The Parent of Tomorrow
Petosiris's Pyramid of Perpetual Wealth
Unlearn the World
Grimoire of the Hollow Tongue
Zodiac Weeds: Finding Your Strain Through the Stars
Aquarius Rises in the Bank
The Sugar God's Smile
The Skinclock Reversal: Biohacking the Face of Time
Debtburn: How to Obliterate What You Owe Forever
The Ice Cream Oracle: What Your Cone Says About Your Future
Silence Is Sovereignty: The Power of Being Unreadable
The Wind That Whispers Through Stone
Path of the Four Directions
Doctor Who: The Maestro's Symphony of Endings
Oxygen Grail: Breathing to Undo the Clock
Zodiacal Collapse: When Stars Devour Time
Teachings from the Red Sand Silence
Doctor Who: Omega – The Broken Equation
Memory Wipe Your Past: Start Over Like a MiB

Mitochondria Prime: Ignite the Core of Youth
A Nest of Roaches
Grub from the Galaxy: MiB Recipes You'll Never Forget
Whiskers of Power: Bastet's Guide to Inner Sovereignty
The Gift Must Cost Them: Negotiation Through Unequal Exchange
The Worm Guys' Wealth Code: Hustle Like an Alien
Bug Out: The Edgar Method for Ruthless Goal Setting
Weaving Life with Spiderwoman's Pattern
Doctor Who: The Rani's Renaissance
How to Get a Job (If You're a Puppygirl)
Speak Through Others: The Art of Proxy Power
T-Rex Your Trauma: Reclaim the Power of Your Primal Self
The Black Briefcase: How MiB Stay Wealthy in Silence
The Thirst Beyond Reason: Understanding Diabetes Insipidus From the Inside Out
Backwoods Witchcraft for Billionaires: The Pagan Path from Dirt Roads to Gold Roads
The Moonshine Grimoire: Fermented Spells for Abundance
The Nameless Geometry
The Wraith's Mixtape: Spellcasting with Songs of Sorrow
The Gallifreyan Gentleman: Silent Wealth, Sonic Confidence, and the Doctor's Code of Living
Sugar Water Confidence
Dino Totems: Spirit Guides from Earth's First Gods
Pumpkin Sigils & Ritual Smoke
The Hózhó Compass
The Distortus Discipline – Order from Inner Mutation
Witchcraft for the Cold-Blooded Soul
Moonlight Over the Blessingway
Water, Interrupted: When the Body Forgets How to Hold On
Deformed but Divine: Embracing Your Asymmetry
Hexes in the Henhouse: The Farm Witch's Guide to Power

The Reversed Flame: A Grimoire of Inverted Power

Salt, Cells, and Sanity: Reclaiming Balance with Diabetes Insipidus

King of the Broken: Crowning the Flawed Self

Moonlight Scars: Emo Moon Magick and the Art of Lunar Sorrow

Noose Spells: Magick of the Hanging Rope

The Goth Cathedral: Rituals of the Broken and Beautiful

The Cretaceous Codex: Dino Spirits and Fossil Magick

The Turkey Bones Ritual

Nine Lives of Manifestation: Unlocking Bastet's Reality Codes

Chaos Muscles: Building Strength from Twisted Pain

Emo Blood Magick: The Veins of Power

The 3AM Flood: Nighttime Urination, Sleep Loss, and the DI Spiral

The Silence Between the Stars

The Lemon Method: Sour Your Way to Success

Starlit Sovereign

The Rite of Twelve Gates: Walking the Gates of the Duat.

Cornbread and Conjure: Recipes for Riches and Rootwork

The Black Rose Rituals: Emo Love Spells and Obsession Magick

The Eternal Goodbye: Death Magick and Rebirth Rituals

Sinkrot: The Drain That Remembers

The Hybrid Mindset: Thinking Beyond Evolution

Bone Dry: Navigating Dehydration Before It Breaks You

Wreathcraft: Winter Sigils and Yuletide Spells

The Rite of Twelve Mouths

S'mores of the Damned: Haunted Recipes for Halloween Night

Rethink the Drink: A Beverage Survival Guide for DI Warriors

The Shadow Chord: Guitar Magick and Sonic

Malformed Yet Majestic: Leading When You Feel Wrong Inside

The Cursed Diary: Ink-Stained Spells of the Emo Soul

Anxiety Off Switch: Emergency Reset for a Fried Nervous System

The Energy Heist: How to Take Back Your Life from Drainers

Beyond the Bathroom: Rebuilding Your Social Life With DI

Coyote's Gift for Decision Makers

Ghoul-Goo: Spooky S'mores You'll Die For

Echoes in the Mirror: Scrying and Self-Destruction Magick

Thread and Thorn: Stitching Spells from Rural Cloth

The Mogwai Mind: Building Untouchable Wealth from Small Ideas

Be Your Own Guide: Trust Your Inner Compass

Hormones in Chaos: The Endocrine Puzzle of Diabetes Insipidus

ChronoCleanse: Detox Your Biological Timeline

The Limb You Hide Is the One That Saves You

Leaves, Bones, and Whisper Spells

The Dinosaur Mindset: Prehistoric Tactics for Modern Wealth

Clawing Back Control: A Bastet Method for Boundaries and Empowerment

Samhain Codes of the Forgotten

Orange Alchemy: The Autumnal Spellbook

Monster Within, Master Without

The Sigil That Sleeps

Hearthcraft: Yule Hearth Sigils and Winter Warmth Spells

Temple of the Purring Moon: Rituals from Bastet's Lineage

When the Earth Remembers Your Footsteps

Food for Mood: Eat to Heal Depression, Not Just Survive It

Witch of the Kudzu Vine: Southern Pagan Wealth Secrets

The Invisible Diagnosis: Advocating for Yourself With DI

The Coffin's Lullaby: Sleep Magick and Nightmares as Portals
Ashes of the Will: Rituals for Erasing the Self
The Fracture Rite: Shattering the Magickal Core
Funeral Candles: The Art of Emo Flame Magick
The Black Grimoire: A Blank Ritual for Writing in Absence
Phantom Thirst: A Halloween Survival Guide for Diabetes Insipidus
The Hollow Crown: Emo Royalty and Magick of the Outcast King
Sandpainting for the Soul
Falling Into Balance: Using the Extra Hour to Recalibrate Life
100 Southern Superstitions That Still Work
The DI Child: A Parent's Guide to Raising Hydrated, Happy Kids
The Jungle of Shame: Escaping the Hidden Lab of Doubt
The Witch's Toast: S'mores Spells and Creepy Confections
The Hoodoo Pantry: Spells from the Mason Jar
The Immortal Fortune: Secret Wealth Lessons from Captain Jack Harkness
The Specter's Embrace: Magick for Channeling Ghostly Lovers
Grateful Waters: A Thanksgiving Survival Guide for Diabetes Insipidus
The Seizure Gospel
Harvestbind: Autumn Sigils and Samhain Spells
Doctor Who: The Algorithmic Awakening
Silent Nights, Steady Waters: A Christmas Survival Guide for Diabetes Insipidus
The Extra Hour Effect: How One Hour Can Transform Everything
Blade Between the Breaths
Running with the Mountain Shadows
Echoes of the Failed Experiment – Becoming a Living Legacy

Swamp Witches & River Ghosts: Real Southern Hauntings

Cornbread Prophecies: Magical Recipes from a Southern Table

Doctor Who: The Signal in the Star

Bloomcraft: Spring Sigils and Equinox Enchantments

Vanisher: How to Disappear from the Internet Without Losing Your Life

The Ultimate Christmas Cookie Cookbook

The Unbreakable Parent: How to Mentally Survive Raising Kids in a Broken World

Time Debt: How to Reclaim the Hours You Didn't Know You Lost

One Month, One Million: Unconventional Cash Creation Tactics

Doctor Who: The Cyber Conversion Protocol

Black Friday Frenzy: The Art of Finding Hidden Online Deals

The Grimoire Buried Under the Apple Tree

Digital Couponing Masterclass: Your Step-by-Step Guide to Black Friday Savings

The Fire Inside the Flint

Shadows on the Ceiling: The Emo Guide to Astral Magick

The Bone-Eaters Beneath Us

Black Friday Bundle Blueprint: Creating Irresistible Product Packages for Maximum Sales

Thirteen Nights of Unbinding

Doctor Who: Engines of Influence

Pumpkin Spice Alchemy: Recipes of Fire and Frost

When Raptor Met Rexy: Prehistoric Lessons in Wild Romance

Oblivion's Candle: Burn the Path Behind You

Campfire Curses and Chocolate: A Halloween S'mores Grimoire

The Wallet That Wasn't Mine: Breaking Free from Inherited Scarcity

The Cola Zodiac: What Your Fizz Says About Your Fate

Frostfire Fortune: Unlocking Winter's Hidden Prosperity

Signal Jamming: Detox Your Brain from Info Overload

The Dust of the Forgotten Rite

The Golden Cat Sigils: Drawing Power in Bastet's Name

Mud Magick: The Prosperity of Getting Dirty

Savory Spicefall: Beyond the Pumpkin Pie

Pumpkin Spice Apothecary Kitchen

The Pumpkin Spice Economy: Turning Trends into Billions

The Ember Veil: 13 Nights of Fire Magick

Financial Freeze: When Earning Triggers Panic

The Gingerbread Alchemist: Sweet Recipes with a Twist

Biosynth Power: Programming Yourself from Scratch

Echoes from the Talking Circle

Truffle Alchemy: Fungus of Fortune

Spores of Power: The Truffle Witch's Handbook

Doctor Who: The Tower That Speaks

The Mycelium Veil: Truffle Magick Unbound

Broke But Ashamed: Healing the Shame Wound of Debt

The Evergreen Mind: Growth Through Winter Stillness

The Black Veil Truffle Rite

The Voice Beneath Symbols

Witchlight on the Bayou: Swamp Spells for Sovereignty

I Grew Up Poor and Now I Sabotage My Success

The Lantern of Hollow Souls

Shutdown Survival: A Citizen's Guide to Thriving When Government Stops

When Abundance Feels Like a Threat: Healing the Hidden Fears of Enough

The Scarecrow Grimoire

Owls of the October Veil

Candlewax and Curses: A Halloween Spellbook

Excavating the Inner Fossil – Transforming Fossilized Thoughtforms into Tools of Power

The Yule Witch's Spellbook: Magick for the Holiday Season

Haunted Christmas: Ghost Stories for Winter Nights

The Christmas Survival Guide: Thriving Through the Chaos

The Bone Orchard Rites

Haunted Commerce: The Ghost in the Marketplace

When Money Triggers the Inner Child

Silent Night with the Silence: A Christmas Thriller

The Lightning Crown: Living and Leading Through Seizures

TARDIS Tidings: Festive Stories from the Whoniverse

Autumn Reset: Slowing Down Without Falling Behind

The Trillion Dollar Soul: Rewriting the Currency of Reality

Truffle Eclipse Magick

Micro-Manifestations: Quick Magick That Works

5-Minute Rituals for Busy Witches

The Marshmallow Massacre: Halloween Treats with a Sinister Twist

Blood and Blackberry Thorns

Magickal Mornings: Rituals for a Blessed Christmas Day

Embers of the All-Hallows Fire

The Pumpkin Market Collapse

The Hour You Gained: Transforming Time Into Power

The Chamber Must Be Sealed: Mastering the Power of Controlled Access

The Cursed Manuscript of Petosiris

The Festive Hearth: Creating Holiday Traditions

Darkness Rising: Thriving as Nights Grow Longer

Harvesting Time: Turning the Year's End Into Your New Beginning

Petosiris and the 13th Zodiac Key

Wagewound: When Paychecks Become Identity Prisons

Walls That Watch

The Silent Feast: Rituals of Power in the Longest Night

The Distortus Legacy : Becoming a Deformed King in a Perfect World

The Hollow Masks

The Gratitude Furnace: Forging Gold from Thanks

Feast of Inner Gold: Eating for Energy and Enlightenment

Haunted Commerce: The Season of Spending Spirits

Fear Bonds: How Panic Creates Profit

Black Friday E-Commerce Playbook: Sales Tactics to Skyrocket Your Holiday Revenue

Budgeting for Black Friday: A Holiday Savings Planner

Haunting the Harvest Moon

The Warrior's Water: Emergency Preparedness for People With DI

The First Sip of the Year: A New Year's Survival Guide for Diabetes Insipidus

Doctor Who: The Thirteenth Node

The Unseen Struggle: Mental Health, Anxiety, and Chronic Thirst

The Hearth's Hidden Ledger: Counting Energies as Currency

The Gift Alchemist: Turning Any Offering Into Gold

The Papyrus of the Bound Spirit

The Magick of Leftovers: Transmutation in the Fridge

Frost and Fortune: Christmas Wealthcraft for the Modern Magus

Last-Minute Gifts: Creative Ideas on a Budget

10 Secrets to Surviving Holiday Crowds

The Witch's Dow Jones

The Witches' Graveyard Shift

Pumpkin Sigils: Carving Rites for Midnight Power

The Secret Shopper's Black Friday Guide: How to Get Early Access and VIP Deals

Fever in the Foundation

The Neuralyzer Reset: Reprogram Your Morning Routine

Lightning Lessons of the White Painted Woman

The Enchanted Snowflake

The Magic Sip: Surviving Disney Parks with Diabetes Insipidus

The One Who Draws Through You

Santa's Secrets: A Magical Holiday Planner

Silent Bells, Loud Miracles: Self-Help for the Season of Stillness

The Sugar Spell Codex: Confectionary Magick of Christmas

Autumn Hexcraft: Fallen Leaves, Fallen Barriers

Sleep Like a Fortress: Build a Life Where Insomnia Can't Survive

Nowhere Was Ever Home

Christmas Under the Stars: A Celestial Holiday Guide

Rentproof: How to Never Be Evicted Again

Workless: Escape the 9-5 Without Being Broke

The Gilded Gift: A Wealth Altar for Christmas Morning

The Black Friday Grimoire

The Hollowing: Ceremonies of Spiritual Collapse

Doctor Who: The Nameless Signal

Where the Eagle Hides His Courage

The Dwarf Tyrant's Ascent: Claiming Power in a World of Giants

The Currency of the Dead: Trading with Spectral Bankers

The Icebound Witch: Survival and Magick in the Cold

The Emergency Money Mind: Constant Crisis, Zero Calm

Thirst & Roses: A Valentine's Survival Guide for Diabetes Insipidus

Springing Into Clarity: Mastering the Energy Shift of Daylight Saving

Speed of the Nanotyrant: Agile Strategies for Life's Hunt

The 90-Day Reset: A Science-Backed Guide to Reinvent Yourself Before the New Year

The Coil of Thorns

Timegates Unleashed

Dopamine Fasting 2.0: Rewiring Your Brain in a World of Overstimulation

The Nanotyrannus Mutation: Embracing Your Differentiated Form

Unwritten January: How to Use the Blank Page of the Year to Re-Author Your Life

Feast of the Forgotten Spirits: Ancestor Magick for the Holidays

The Burnout Codex: A System for Thriving Beyond Stress

I Don't Deserve to Have Money

When the King Doesn't See You: The Shadow Predator's Guide

The Reset Ritual :A Guide to Shedding Last Year's Weight—Emotional and Physical—by Spring Cleaning Your Soul

Calendar Alchemy: Learn to Bend Time and Productivity around Your Natural Rhythms

The Mirror Contract: A One-Sentence Agreement with Yourself that Unlocks Real Change

The Nile Formula: Sacred Flow for Millionaire Minds

Forward Momentum: Productivity Rituals for the Lost Hour

Harvest Gold: Wealth Magick of Pumpkin Spice Commerce

The Magick of Christmas Lights: Illuminating Holiday Rituals

Cranberry Crown: Royal Self-Worth through Ritual Meals

Petosiris and the Worms of the Feathered Throne

The Evergreen Equation: Self-Help for Sustained Growth

The Rain Will Wash Us Away: Emo Weather Magick

Snowlight Shadows: Magick Under Frozen Stars

Doctor Who: Merger of Empires

The Light Within the Feast: Magickal Wealth of Yuletide Flame

Momentum Machines: Small Habits Designed to Snowball into Unstoppable Forward Motion

Calm Spells: Magickal Solutions for Anxiety Relief

Santa's Final List: The Naughty Never Leave

The Mystic's Guide to Banishing Worry

The Silence Dividend: Turning Quiet Mornings into Compounding Growth All Year

Charmed Stillness: Rituals to Ease the Mind

Blood Spiral Ascension

The Vanishing Heart Invocation

Crystal Calm: Harnessing Stones for Anxiety

The Nano Tyrant Code: Strength in the Small Predator

The Energy Ledger: Accounting Methods for Vitality, Not Just Money

Snowglobe Mindset: Shake Up Your Thoughts, Settle Into Peace

The Weight of the Feather: Anubis's Codes for Soul Balance

Pocket Peppermint Power: Tiny Rituals for Big Holiday Energy

Shadowkeeper of the Golden Jackal: Anubis's Path to Energetic Protection

The Witch's Breath: Anxiety Relief Through Magickal Breathing

The Tiny Ember: Pocket Motivation for Cold Days

Stocking Sorcery: Mini Spells for Holiday Luck and Prosperity

Warm Hands, Steady Heart: Micro Grounding for Winter Anxiety

The Jackal's Lantern: Guide-Lights for Walking the Dark Path

Anubis's Silent Steps: Rituals for Stealth, Peace & Emotional Quiet

The Bonewake Protocol

Extinction-Proof: How to Outlive Trends, Trauma, and Time

The Fourth Doctor: The Eccentric Wanderer

The Second Doctor: Chaos and Charm in the TARDIS (Patrick Troughton, 1966–1969)

The Third Doctor: Earthbound Defender of Time (Jon Pertwee, 1970–1974)

The First Doctor: Genesis of the Time Lord (William Hartnell, 1963–1966)

The Fourth Doctor: The Eccentric Wanderer *(Tom Baker, 1974–1981)*

The Fifth Doctor: Elegance and Empathy (Peter Davison, 1982–1984)

The Sixth Doctor: A Kaleidoscope of Conflict (Colin Baker, 1984–1986)

The Seventh Doctor: The Strategist of Shadows (Sylvester McCoy, 1987–1989)

The Eighth Doctor: A Time Lord's Renaissance (Paul McGann, 1996)

The War Doctor: A Time Lord's Burden (John Hurt, 2013)

The Ninth Doctor: The Healer of Worlds
(Christopher Eccleston, 2005)

The Tenth Doctor: The Lonely Hero (David Tennant, 2005–2010)

The Eleventh Doctor: The Madman in a Box (Matt Smith, 2010–2013)

The Twelfth Doctor: The Rebel with a Cause (Peter Capaldi, 2013–2017)

The Thirteenth Doctor: Breaking the Mold
(Jodie Whittaker, 2017–2022)

The Fourteenth Doctor: A New Beginning (David Tennant, 2022–2023)

The Fifteenth Doctor: Rewriting the Stars
(Ncuti Gatwa, 2023–2025)
Santa's Shortcut to Success: Micro Habits for a Better New Year
The Midnight Cocoa Manifesto: Comfort Rituals for Hard Nights
Why I Can't Save: Trauma Blocks to Financial Planning
Dino Brain, Mega Goals: Rewire Yourself for Savage Success.
Jurassic Profit: Unearth Your Inner Millionaire Fossil
Scales & Softness: Dating with Dino Heart
Carnotaurus Dreams.
Red Willow Thinking.
Reindeer Resilience: How to Keep Going When You're Exhausted
Candlewick Courage: Lighting Strength in Dark Seasons.
Elf-Mode Focus: Fast Attention Fixes for Busy Seasons
Futureproof Feelings: Emotional Skill-Building for Resilience No Matter What the New Year Brings
The 90-Day Rewire: Transform Your Neural Pathways Before Spring Blooms
Jolly Rich: Christmas Micro-Money Magick for Fast Prosperity.
Gingerbread Gratitude: Mini Practices for a Happier Holiday
Trauma-Spending: When Money Becomes a Drug
Goal Skeletons: Build Minimalist Frameworks for Resolutions That Last
The Snarl Strategy: Growling Back at a World That Silenced You
The Hourglass Reset: Reclaiming What the Clock Took
Yule Claw: Dino Rites of Light in the Darkness
Sacred Circles: Grounding Rituals for Anxious Souls
Clockstopper's Gut: Rebuilding the Core of Time

Winterfire Drive: Harness the Cold Season's Stillness to Ignite Deep Motivation

The 5-Minute Productivity Hack: Small Steps to Big Results

Light Ascending: A Self-Help Guide to Longer Days

Inner Economy: Trade Self-Doubt for Confidence Like a High-Value Currency

Simple Success: Decluttering Your Life for Better Results

The Resilient Mind: Thriving in Tough Times

The 2026 Playbook: Mastering the Year Ahead

The Spring Sleep Solution: Conquering Fatigue After Time Change.

The Hormonal Compass: Navigate Back to Your Youth

Golden Vision: Eating for Your Eye Color with the Power of Ghee

Lionhearted Love: Strength in Relationships

MiB Mindset: Think Like a Cosmic Agent

The Ladder of Small Wins: Climb Out of Stagnation by Stacking Micro-Victories

The Momentum Hour: Gaining More in Less Time.

The Year of You: A Self-Help Blueprint for Unapologetic Self-Ownership

The Dust That Watches You Back.

The Astral Parent

Shadow of the King: The Nanotyrannus Parable

Tiny Tidings of Triumph: Small Wins That Change Your Life

Dwarf Tyrant Rising: When You're the One They Overlook

The Bank Account Mirror: Healing How You See Yourself Through Money

Cretaceous Black

When Love Costs Too Much: Romantic Triggers and Financial Wounds

Dream-Eater's Guide to Wealth

Unzipped Reality: The Jacket That Opens Portals

The Power of No: How to Set Boundaries and Get Rich

Keeper of the Desert Veil: Anubis's Teachings on Illusion & Truth

Redacted Stargates: Stories the SGC Buried

The Clock That Dripped Time

Doctor Who: The Silent Acquisition

Hairline Manifestation: Unlocking Power at the Edge of Thought

Cash-Eater Crickets: How Insects Predict Economic Collapse

Dead Pet Whisperer: Grief Alchemy from the Other Side

The Love Algorithm Is Broken: Hack Romance Before It Hacks You

The Rite of the 8-Limbed Seal

Melt the Moon: A Fire Ritual to Reshape Emotion

Venomous Miracles: Healing Through the Poison Path

Wealth Without Water: The Post-Aquatic Rich Life

The Butterfly Betrayal: When Change Turns on You

The Quiet Upgrade: How Humans Are Secretly Rebuilding Themselves Without Asking Permission

Nobody Taught Us This: The Missing Human Manual for Money, Energy, and Self-Respect

You Were Never Broken: Why Most People Are Reacting Normally to an Unstable World

After the Noise Ends: How Humans Reset When the World Finally Goes Quiet

The Month That Tells the Truth: Why January Reveals What the Rest of the Year Hides

Tremors Party Unleashed: The Ultimate Guide to a Graboids Birthday Bash

Cold Start Human: Rebooting Motivation Without Forcing Momentum

The Year that doesn't start until they say

Love Without Performance: What Connection Looks Like When No One Is Watching

February Is a Mirror: What Love Exposes About You

How We Learned Love Wrong: Uninstalling Cultural Myths About Connection

You Are Not Too Much: Why Needing Love Is Not a Flaw

The Crooked Fence Covenant: Backwoods Boundaries and Witch Wealth

The Day That Keeps Repeating: Why Your Life Feels Stuck—and How to Shift It Gently

Nothing Changes Until Something Softens: Escaping Repetition Without Violence to Yourself

Same Life, Different Ending: How Tiny Choices Rewrite Repetition

The Loop Isn't Punishment: Why You're Being Asked to Learn, Not Suffer

Panic at the Register: Retail Anxiety and Public Shame

The Secret Formula to Becoming an Influencer in 90 Days

The New Rich: How to Retire by 35

Digital Nomad Secrets: How to Travel the World and Make Millions

Burn Your Waiting Room: Escape the Delay Spiral

Strapped for Pleasure: A Complete Guide to Pegging and Strap-On Play

Locked in Desire: A Guide to Chastity Play and Intimate Control

Burrowing into History: Groundhog Day Through the Ages

The Shadow Forecast: The Science of Groundhog Day

Choice Cascades: How One Decision in January Sets Ripples for the Whole Year

The Anti-Anxiety Blueprint: Mastering Fear and Stress for Success

The Ancestral Path of the Jackal Priest

Winterborn Titans: Giants of Ice and Stone

The Extinction Spire

The Emotion That Made Me Millions

Delete Their Voice: Become Unreachable

The Frostbound Mysteries: Mythical Beings of January's Chill

The Roar Within: Unlocking Your Potential

From Burrow to Sky: Groundhog Day Explained

The Boogey Book: Festive Ward-Off Edition

Fooled Ya! The Psychology Behind Great Pranks

April Fools' Alchemy: Transforming Everyday Items into Pranks

Anchor Habits: Root Yourself in Unshakable Routines That Endure Seasonal Change

Emerald Waters: A St. Patrick's Day Survival Guide for Diabetes Insipidus

The Groundhog's Legacy: Myths, Legends, and Facts

Six Weeks of Mystery: The Truth Behind Groundhog Day

The Upgrade Mind: Tech-Like Patches and Updates for Your Mental Operating System

Moon Blood, Star Flesh: Embracing Your Hybrid Nature

Groundhog Lore and Legend: A Complete Guide

You Are the Lie They Can't Kill

Download a Different Reality

The Quiet Advantage: Winning Without Announcing Yourself

A Year of Gratitude: Unlocking Joy

Touch Grass: A Pagan Reset for a Burned-Out Digital World

Cold Start Wealth: Building Financial Power from a Standing Still Point

Astrology Without Fate: Using Cycles Without Surrendering Control

The Future is Remote: Work Less, Earn More, Live Anywhere

Harvest of Silence

The Algorithm Knows Your Name
April Fools' Day for Introverts
Soft Power Systems: Influence That Doesn't Exhaust You
Practical Magick for Real Life: Focus, Intent, and Follow-Through
January Is a Lie: Designing Momentum Without the Calendar
Universal Flow: Managing DI in High-Energy Theme Parks
Electric Allure: Exploring Erotic Electro-Play
The Masked Embrace: Exploring Sensory Deprivation
The Ultimate April Fools' Survival Guide
Splashproof Survival: Waterparks & Wave Pools with DI
Agile Predator, Still King: Crafting Your Speed in a World That Celebrates Size
The Shadow Feast: Groundhog Day's Sinister Side
The Bug's Business Model
Edge of Bliss: Mastering the Art of Tease and Denial
Midnight Alchemy: Rituals for Transformation Between the Old Year and the New
Punxsutawney Bloodlines: A Groundhog Day Horror
The Burrower: Groundhog Day's Darkest Secrets
Buried Alive: A Groundhog Day Horror Story
Blood Moon Markets: The Witch's Guide to Wealth Magick
The Groundhog's Shadow: What It Means for the World
Seasonal Shadows: The Groundhog Day Phenomenon
The Shadow's Curse: A Groundhog Day Horror Tale
Punxsutawney Revealed: A Guide to Groundhog Day
Safari Hydration: Zoo & Wildlife Park Survival for DI
The Foolproof Prank Planner
Latex Lust: Embracing Fetish Fashion **is a sophisticated**
Whip & Whisper: The Dynamics of Impact Play
The Shadow Burrow Chronicles: Horror Beneath the Ground
Frozen Shadows: A Groundhog Day Thriller
The Groundhog's Revenge: A February Nightmare

Burrow of the Damned
Everyday Enchantment: Magickal Practices for Modern Living
Budget Bliss: The Easy Path to Financial Freedom
Six More Weeks of Terror
The Oxygen Debt
The Ice Veil: Mystical Beasts of January's Shadows
Roots That Remember
Polar Myths: Creatures of the Icy Abyss
The Marginalia Covenant
AI and the Occult: Digital Spirits, Sigils, and Cyber-Witchcraft
Roleplay Realms: Crafting Fantasies and Scenes
The Last Clean River
Lover in the Shadows: A Groundhog Day Tale
Buried Hearts: A Groundhog Day Gothic Romance
Anubis Wept for Petosiris
The Lantern Knows Your Name
Rituals of the Last Shadow
The Bell That Rings for No One
Shadows of Love and Death
The Groundhog's Bride: A Dark Valentine's Tale
Frozen Kisses: A Horror Romance for Groundhog Day
The Creative Spark: Igniting Your Passion Projects
From Cub to King: A Journey of Transformation
Six Weeks to Midnight: A Groundhog Day Romance
Tide of the Unclean
Burrow of Desire: A Groundhog Day Paranormal Romance
The Shadow Magick Almanac: Harnessing Groundhog Day Energies
AI for Emo Influencers: Growing an Online Following Without the Anxiety
AI for the Melancholy Millionaire: Making Money Without Social Interaction

Winter's Grip: A Horror Romance Beneath the Frost

Shadowed Hearts: A Love Buried in Winter's Chill

The Shadow Lover: A Groundhog Day Gothic Love Story

Beneath the Burrow: A Groundhog Day Thriller

The Punxsutawney Conspiracy

The Crimson Pact: Emo Blood Oath Magick

The Shadows of Gallifrey: A Doctor Who Horror Collection

Whispers in the Vortex: Chilling Tales from the TARDIS

AI Ghostwriting for Emo Souls: How to Make Money Writing Without Trying

The Anti-Social Emo's Guide to AI-Powered Freelancing

Emo AI Therapy: Talking to Robots When Humans Suck

Cry & Collect: AI-Powered Passive Income for Emos

The Weeping Angel Chronicles: A Collection of Terror

Dating Without the Mask

The Clockwork Menace: Horror Stories from the Future

Tender Doesn't Mean Weak

Not a Burden, Not a Bonus

Dalek Nightmares: Stories of Ultimate Extermination

The Empty Child's Curse: Tales of Horror and Fear

The TARDIS Ghost Files: Hauntings Across the Universe

Soft Armor, Open Heart

Chosen Gently

Love That Doesn't Rush You

***Financial Gaslighting: When You're Made to Feel Crazy About Money*.**

After the Bees Went Silent

The Soil Knows Your Name

The Quantum Magick Codex: Unlocking the Hidden Laws of Reality

The Gingerbread Golem's Awakening: A Tale of Sweet Revenge

The Gingerbread Golem Chronicles: Guardians of Frost Hollow

The Power of Focus: Eliminate Distractions, Achieve Greatness

Sacred Submission: The Dynamics of D/s Relationships

The Magick of Numbers: Unlocking the Hidden Codes of the Universe

Blood and Bones: The Ancient Magick of Life and Death

Doctor Who: The Collapse Dividend

Thesis of the Unremembered

Desired as You Are

The Energy Budget of Love

Romancing Your Potential: The Love Month Growth Guide

Seen, Not Studied

Screams from the Void: Horror Stories Inspired by Doctor Who

The Silence Is Watching: A Collection of Dread

Under the Floorboards

The House of Feathers and Fangs

Emperor Bones, Hollow Crown

Goreglyphs of the Boiling Deep

The Coven That Screamed Back

The Stacks That Breathe

Love That Adapts

Nightmares on Gallifrey: Frights from the Doctor Who Universe

Apache Ways to Heal Powerfully

Belos Left No Corpses

The Algorithm Hates You (Good.)

Starve the Soul, Feed the Flame

Romance Without Apology

The Carbon Illusion

Your Nervous System is Your GPS

Where Rest Learns Your Name: Six Gentle Bedtime Stories for Minds That Work Differently

Soft Armor for Tender Nights: Six 5-Minute Bedtime Stories for Hearts That Have Been Hurt

Paws of Night, Path of Stars: Six 5-Minute Bedtime Stories Guided by Bastet and Anubis

When the Mind Needs a Lamp: Six 5-Minute Bedtime Stories for Gentle Mental Health Care

Imbolc Roar: Awakening the Dino Flame

The Titan Never Died

Witchflesh Harvest

Become the Thought They Can't Unsee

Golden Threads: The Sensuality of Body Worship

Chains of Desire: Exploring the Beauty of Restraint

Glyphs Written in Organs

Living Below the Line

Palismen Don't Scream—Until They Do

The Boiling Isles Devour the Weak

Hexside Anatomy Lab

Philip Wittebane and the First Body

Money PTSD: When Trauma Hijacks Your Finances

Brother, Bone, and Betrayal

Lipstick Like a Weapon: A Goth Girl's Guide to Emotional Dominance, Boundaries, and Quiet Intimidation

The Scar Is the Portal

Don't Grow—Mutate

Built from Breakdown: The Collapse Code

The Collector's First Lesson

Glyph Failure Syndrome

Philip Wittebane and the Discipline of Lies

The Making of Belos

Flesh Does Not Belong

The Golden Guard Prototypes

Coven Marks as Control Wounds
The Voice Belos Invented
The Boogeyman Within: Shadow Work for Personal Transformation
The Energy Edge: Reclaiming Your Power
Mindful March: A Quick Guide to Intentional Living
Love on Autopilot: Rekindle Your Relationship Instantly
Spring Renewal: Refresh Your Mindset Before the Equinox
Velvet Control: The Subtle Art of Erotic Choking
Erotic Shadows: Playing with Voyeurism and Exhibitionism
The Green Pulse Awakens
Equinox Bones
Immortality Is a Disease
Cold-Blooded Focus
The Invasive Advantage
The Lonely Assassin's Love: A Weeping Angel Romance
Philip Is Still Inside
Become the Signal That Replaces the Noise
When the Soil Says Yes
Shedding What No Longer Protects You
The Shadow Key: Unlocking the Power of Your Dark Self
The Enchanted Chocolate Rituals: Magickal Recipes for Love & Wealth
Love in the Vortex: A Doctor Who Horror Romance
Grimwalker Number Seventeen
The Boy Who Woke Again
Sad Girls Don't Beg: Reclaiming Self-Worth When Melancholy Is Mistaken for Weakness
Raising Pagan Children in a Non-Pagan World
The Pagan Homeschool Exit Strategy
Protecting Childhood While Preparing for Adulthood
Curriculum for the Dead
Too Much for Who? Reclaiming the Power of Intensity

Your Nervous System Is the Algorithm
Memories That Don't Belong to Him
The Golden Guard Template
Time-Locked Hearts: A Gallifreyan Gothic Romance
Ostara's Hatchlings: Fertile Dino Magick
The Dalek's Heart: A Tale of Forbidden Love
The Jackal's Final Game
Where Wild Magic Took My Brother
Where Love Meets Reality
Volume Without Apology
The Mind of Stillness: Petosiris's Hidden Teachings on Power
Doctor Who: The Final Shareholder Meeting
The Archive of Unfinished Lives
AI for Emo Musicians: Automating Your Sad Soundtracks
AI-Generated Emo Art: Selling Melancholy in Digital Form
Ashes Where the Cathedral Slept
The Monarch of Splintered Wings
People-Pleasing Is a Survival Strategy Past Its Expiration Date
Velvet Carnage Covenant
The Intensity Advantage
Attention Is a Finite Resource—You're Overspending It
Emotional Debt Compounds Faster Than Money
The Siege of Thornlit Graves
When the Bone King Wept Black
Comfort Is the Most Expensive Addiction
The AI Gothpreneur: Building a Business Without Any Social Interaction
AI & Tarot: Emo Divination for the Digital Age
Sad AI Aesthetics: Emo Branding & Personal Style
Black Sails Over a Dying Sun
The Crimson Parliament of Wolves
Cathedral of Veins and Thunder
The Orchard of Hanging Saints

The Self-Discovery Path: Find Your True Purpose
You Were Taught to Self-Sabotage Politely
Chrysalis Debt: Reborn into Wealth
Empire of Teeth and Perfume
The Devourer's Bride of Iron Mist
The Dormitory with No Windows
Built Larger Than the Room
The Silence Between Wings
The Manuscript That Grades You
The Librarian Who Refused to Die
Footnotes for a Burning Campus
The Thornblood Accord
The Paranormal Files: True Encounters with Ghosts, Aliens, and the Unexplained
Warfare in the Temple of Shattered Constellations
The Crow's Codex: Unlocking the Secrets of the Black-Winged Messengers
Purring Boundaries: Bastet's Guide to Raising Fierce Children
The Arcane Wealth Formula: Spellcasting for Infinite Abundance
The Celestial Spellbook: Harnessing Planetary Magick for Power and Fortune
Silk Shrouds of the Frostbound Wilds
Windtalker: The Hill Witch's Guide to Whisper Magick
The Doctrine of Psyence: Knowledge Beyond the Veil
The Bone Sovereign's Final War Chant
The Abyssal Altar of Salt and Silver
The Lantern Wilds That Devoured Lovers
The Court of the Sable Scar
Wax & Whispers: The Art of Candle Play